The
Millionairess
Across the Street

Bettina Flores &
Jennifer Basye Sander

Dearborn
Financial Publishing, Inc.®
A Kaplan Professional Company

This publication is designed to provide accurate and authoritative information in regard to the subject matter covered. It is sold with the understanding that the publisher is not engaged in rendering legal, financial, accounting, or other professional service. If legal advice or other expert assistance is required, the services of a competent professional should be sought.

Editorial Director: Cynthia Zigmund
Managing Editor: Jack Kiburz
Project Editor: Trey Thoelcke
Interior Design: Lucy Jenkins
Cover Design: Design Alliance, Inc.
Typesetting: the dotted i

© 1999 by Bettina R. Flores and Jennifer Basye Sander

Published by Dearborn Financial Publishing, Inc.®

All rights reserved. The text of this publication, or any part thereof, may not be reproduced in any manner whatsoever without written permission from the publisher.

Printed in the United States of America

99 00 01 10 9 8 7 6 5 4 3 2

Library of Congress Cataloging-in-Publication Data
Flores, Bettina.
    The millionairess across the street / Bettina R. Flores and Jennifer Basye Sander.
        p.   cm.
    Includes bibliographical references and index.
    ISBN 0-7931-3167-7 (pbk.)
    1. Women millionaires—United States.   2. Success in business—United States.   I. Sander, Jennifer Basye, 1958–   .   II. Title.
    HC110.W4F55   1999
    332.014′042—dc21   98-33219
                                                                        CIP

Dearborn books are available at special quantity discounts to use as premiums and sales promotions, or for use in corporate training programs. For more information, please call the Special Sales Manager at 800-621-9621, ext. 4514, or write to Dearborn Financial Publishing, Inc., 155 North Wacker Drive, Chicago, IL 60606-1719.

CONTENTS

I·NTRODUCTION

Welcome to *The Millionairess Across the Street,* the first book of its kind about women millionaires, money, and success.

According to statistics, there are about 500,000 women millionaires! Even more impressive, 43 percent of all millionaires are women. So here is a book on women as millionaires, because the exciting news is there's plenty of room for more!

Me? You say. Go from grass roots to major green backs? Become a millionaire? Well, why not?

For many people, the word *millionaire* evokes images of people way, way up there, untouchable, snobby. Forget that. First of all, a million dollars isn't a lot of money anymore. The sometimes soaring stock market has turned many investors into millionaires. Even more exhilarating, a growing force of entrepreneurs is finding tremendous financial rewards for their efforts. Secondly, people are people. Whether they are on welfare or Wall Street. Some are nice, others not so nice.

The Millionairess Across the Street introduces you to women millionaires who have built empires on ideas and dreams. Their grass roots efforts, business ventures, self-determination, and self-reliance give new meaning to the word *millionaire.* These women come from all walks of life and many came to be rich more through their personality traits and passions than through a Harvard MBA! Their astounding dramas—struggles, tragedies, temptations, bankruptcies, divorces—are all a part of their incredible success.

We define our millionairess as a woman who has a net worth of one million dollars. However, because the first million is the hardest to make (and keep) and the world of finance is a relatively new frontier for most women, we also profile women who have built million-dollar enterprises. Some women ride the fast track, others pace themselves for the long haul, and, believe it or not, others fall into being millionaires by accident. Well, whatever it takes!

Every woman who wants freedom, security, power, and a healthy and good quality of life should consider becoming a *millionaire.* It's important to recognize how important money is to women's lives.

Perhaps you're thinking, this book should have been written by a millionaire? Well here's your first lesson in becoming a millionaire: Nothing ventured nothing gained. In true millionaire spirit, Bettina conceived the idea, gave it focus, and ran with it like a renegade. When friend and writer Jennifer joined in, both harmonized: Why not? with double conviction!

Think about this: If women had to "credentialize" their every move, they'd still be sitting at home. This can't be more true than for creative, entrepreneurial-type women who take risk after risk, with only their brains, talent, intuition, and relentless energy as credentials to become millionaires!

Our first step in writing *The Millionairess Across the Street* was to find out what books were already out there and what they said. We found that nearly all the financial books for women that we've read are based on fear—a woman's very real fear of ending up alone and penniless, living on cat food in a shabby apartment in a scary urban area. All these books seem to have the same central message: Take these simple steps now to protect yourself and your future. Television advertising also seems to promote this image. Witness the soft-focus shots of a woman dressed in black, standing tearfully at the edge of a recent grave. Protect yourself and your future.

Protect yourself? Why is it that once again, we women are being frightened into action? The same sort of big business that spends huge amounts of money on advertising to make us frightened that our skin isn't soft enough, that our hair isn't the right color, and that our thighs are too big, also is playing on our fears about poverty to encourage us to buy insurance policies, invest in mutual funds, or buy bonds. Women should make these kinds of investments, of course, but we should not be motivated by fear. We should be motivated by confidence, pride, and a belief in our own ability to handle money.

When *The Millionaire Next Door* was first published, we both read it eagerly. After finishing the book, we thought: Hey, where are the women? The authors seldom used women as examples, and when they did, they were of the "and his thrifty wife shops at Wal-Mart" variety. In that book, most of the millionaires profiled are men who have been in long-term marriages. Now that is great news for their wives, or for any woman who has been married for 20 or so years, but what about the rest of the women in America? Gosh, is being married to a man who owns his own business the only way a woman can build wealth? Haven't any women out there—married or single—built wealth on their own? (Yes, so read on.)

Other negative money attitudes in wide circulation now include the "simplicity" movement and "downscaling" one's lifestyle. Who is buying these books on simplicity in big numbers? Women are. Once again it seems that we are being told, albeit in a warm and fuzzy way, that we should settle for less than we deserve, and not to set our sights too high lest we be disappointed.

So we two, Bettina and Jennifer, your tour guides into the world of women millionaires, both felt that what was missing—not only from the bookstore shelves but from our lives—was positive motivation about accumulating money. As your motivational money coaches, we take a different approach from the financial books already available. We urge this attitude adjustment: Think of *The Millionairess Across the Street* as

- being about *much abundance,* not simple abundance!
- women's answer to the void in *The Millionaire Next Door.*

- teaching you *how to feel better about wanting more* instead of *how to be satisfied settling for less!*

We say, latch on to the central message of *The Millionairess Across the Street*. We believe that women can *enjoy* the process of increasing capital and net worth, that they are *strong enough* to withstand the constant efforts of others to part them from their money, and that they are *confident enough* to take active steps to grow their wealth.

We also want to present you with what women who have become millionaires believe is the key to their success. We went straight to the source—women who are millionaires in their own right—and asked them for advice. We asked them a simple question: "If you could distill your own formula for making money and building wealth down to one thing, one single piece of usable advice for other women, what would it be?" The answers astonished us—as they will you!

In *The Millionairess Across the Street* we, of course, discuss money, money, and more money—millions and billions of dollars. If the bold-as-brass money talk makes you uncomfortable, know that you are not alone. Many women find it easier to talk about sex than money. Don't be embarrassed and don't give up. Hang in there and learn all you can. There is much to gain and celebrate.

Last, you must know this. Once upon a time, being rich meant that you had to own and control timber, oil, real estate, factories, or printing presses—or use Daddy's or Hubby's millions. That was yesterday. Today's fortunes are being made on ideas. And what's the one thing women do best: organize ideas!

You have the gift for becoming a millionaire inside of you. Everyone has a unique God-given talent. Whether that talent stays on the back burner or blossoms to its full potential—millionized—is up to you. Turning the corner to millionaire status requires taking charge. It requires action, and as you are about to witness, it happens across the country every day.

The Millionairess Across the Street contains 23 key lessons. We've kept the book small enough that it can accompany you in your daily routine and be read over and over. The lessons in the first part of the book focus on helping you to "pump up your attitude" about money and success. The second section helps you find ways to "bump up your income." We hope that when you reach the end of *The Millionairess Across the Street,* you will be raring to go out and acquire what you need to live a life of wealth.

If you are interested in accumulating wealth, *The Millionairess Across the Street* is a great place to start. It offers you

- an awareness of how the truly wealthy live and think.
- exciting opportunities to learn from wealthy women.
- an open door to broader thinking and wider visions.
- the challenge to think caviar instead of cornflakes!

ABOUT THE AUTHORS

Bettina R. Flores is a journalist, public speaker, commentator, and seminar leader who, once again, is boldly pioneering new thinking with *The Millionairess Across the Street.*

The author of the best-seller *Chiquita's Cocoon,* Bettina developed the cultural cocoon concept, which explores the traditional status of women. The *Los Angeles Times* hailed this groundbreaking work a "classic." Her early years inspired *Chiquita's Diary,* a young adult novel. She also created the *Chiquita's Diary Teacher Edition.* Both *Chiquitas* are used as textbooks or supplementary readings in education, as well as by health and welfare agencies. Her work has been referenced in many books.

Bettina has been featured by CNN, *New York Times,* NPR, and other media.

Bettina welcomes correspondence. Please indicate whether your letter can be used in workshops, lectures, or subsequent books.

P.O. Box 2037
Granite Bay, CA 95746-2037
916-791-2237
Fax 916-791-8463
E-mail: bettina@quiknet.com

Jennifer Basye Sander is a financial writer and small business owner. The author of 12 published books, she operates Big City Books, a book packaging company. Among the books she wrote are *101 Best Extra Income Opportunities for Women, How to Become a Successful Weekend Entrepreneur,* and *The Complete Idiot's Guide to Getting Published.* Jennifer speaks frequently to writer's groups and women's groups. She lives in Granite Bay, California, with her husband and two small sons.

Jennifer can be reached at

P.O. Box 2463
Granite Bay, CA 95746-2463

LESSON 1

Think Big Now! Think and Build for the Long-Term Payoff

Let's begin where all things start—in the mind. The purpose of this first lesson is to get you mentally focused so that you can achieve your stated goal—to become a millionairess!

From this moment on, and for however long your mission to become a millionairess takes, some of your strongest allies will be three small, but powerful, words: *Think big now.* Believe it, becoming a millionairess is not a test of intelligence. It is more like a test of your will to be mentally tough and believe in yourself through thick and thin. Embrace the words *think big* as your own motivational self-talk, your chant, your mantra. Live by those words, sleep by them, and wake to them every morning. Surrender yourself fully to *thinking big* for it is your path to achieving the million-dollar mark.

What is so magical about the words *think big now?* By imbedding the words *think big now* in the forefront of your thoughts and using them constantly, you provoke both the questions and the answers to "How can I think bigger? How can I do better?

1

How can I make more money?" Your mind will automatically awaken and lift you to a much higher level of thinking, expectation, and success. When you say to yourself, "I can do better," the ways to do better will actually appear. Magic? Not really. It is simply your self-directed decision and your personal commitment and reinforcement that make things happen!

But, you protest, "I do think big! Why must I learn to *think big now?*" Sadly, women have not been encouraged to think big, outrageous money and success thoughts. Even when asked about our wildest dreams, women will shyly offer up visions of a larger house, a newer car, or a luxurious vacation. Surprisingly small desires, given all that is out there in the world.

A remarkable example of this played out on national television. Oprah Winfrey asked women to send her their *three wishes,* and some 77,000 women sent their wishes to her show. The winner, the one with the biggest wish of all? A woman who wanted to take her children to Europe. A wonderful dream, of course, but where were the women who dreamed of being on the board of directors of a major corporation? Where was the woman who wanted her own Learjet? Where were the women who wished to no longer show up at an office every morning at 9:00 AM to help make millions for a company that, in the end, will reward their efforts and creativity with only a small salary and a paltry two weeks of vacation?

Could this be happening because women resist thinking big? Resistance to thinking big manifests itself daily in statements like, "I'm only a woman, I don't have a chance of becoming a millionaire on my own," or "Who would ever loan me start-up money?" Watch out! Resistance to thinking big becomes a self-fulfilling prophecy and will always result in self-defeating behavior. *You need to focus your mind and accept larger ideas constantly.*

You can read how-to book after how-to book but the change you desire—to become a millionairess—will only come when you truly understand and believe in the universal law that everything you are is connected with the thoughts in your mind.

Yes, your entire life—whether you live in a shack or mansion, happily or unhappily—stems from the ideas embedded in your mind. All things start in the mind with thoughts. Thoughts lead to decisions. Decisions lead to actions. And actions lead to results. Let's illustrate:

Thoughts
↓
Decisions
↓
Actions
↓
Results

Developing and achieving millionaire mindpower is no different. You must first entertain the thought of becoming a millionairess. You must decide to become a millionairess. And you must take action to bring forth the results.

Because absolutely everything originates in the mind, what goes on in your mind must be working for you, working toward achieving your goal 24 hours a day. So let's not only think big in general, but in specifics as well. A specific, unfailing, and universal program to motivate and sustain you as you work toward your goals costs nothing, is easy, and goes like this:

- Think big in affirmations.
- Think big in visualization.
- Think big in action.

THINK BIG IN AFFIRMATIONS

The word affirmation means to make firm. Affirmations are statements created and used to program in your mind what you want out of life. Affirmations are a powerful way to help you turn your thoughts into achievements. What your mind can conceive, you can achieve.

THE POWER OF MILLION-DOLLAR AFFIRMATIONS

Because you can only hold one thought in your mind at a time, the use of powerful and positive affirmations keeps you on track and eliminates the useless babble that might otherwise monopolize your thoughts.

You should use affirmations as often and in as many ways as you can. You can set aside a specific meditating time. Make an appointment with yourself and write it into your schedule. You can buy a small tape recorder and record yourself saying your affirmations aloud, then listen to them while you commute. You can stand in front of the mirror and say your affirmations out loud. You can write your affirmations down on three-by-five-inch index cards and carry them with you always. Instead of constantly thinking of your worries, frustrations, or the petty problems of day-to-day life, why not let positive million-dollar affirmations dominate your thoughts? Their value is priceless. Here are three sample affirmations. Use these to get started now and then write your own.

1. I am a powerful, effective woman who thinks big!
2. I am a strong woman in command of my life and my financial future!
3. I am well on my way to my first million dollars!

THINK BIG IN VISUALIZATION

Scientists tell us that we only use 10 percent of our minds. Imagine what we could do if we used the other 90 percent! Scientists also tell us that we don't process information in words or thoughts, but rather in pictures. Imagine, pictures! Put the power of visualization to work and begin to see yourself as a millionairess.

Close your eyes right now. Can you see yourself as a millionairess? Clearly and in great detail? Get creative in the pictures that you conjure up—try to picture a bank statement with your name on it that shows a balance of a million dollars. Remember: *Think big!* Close your eyes and imagine seven-figure contracts with your name on the signature line, a phone call from a large company offering you a million-dollar deal, or even a UPS truck filled with orders for a million dollars worth of your product! Visualize big, and visualize often! Make an appointment with yourself to visualize just as often as you say your affirmations. A great time to visualize is just before drifting off to sleep. Who knows what kinds of creative thoughts might fill your dreams?

THINK BIG IN ACTION

Nothing gets you to the top faster than giant leaps. In the spirit of thinking big, ponder this: Why be a babysitter when you can be a day-care owner? Why be an unpaid volunteer when you can be on the board of directors? Why sell into a niche market when the mass market is, uh, massive? Why stay with just one store when you can franchise? And, extremely important for women, why give away your ideas when you can patent, copyright, trademark, or license them?

A perfect example of thinking big in action is the business movement known as *cobranding*. Walk into a Barnes and Noble bookstore almost anywhere in the nation and chances are you will find a Starbucks coffee café inside. Start your day with Dunkin' Donuts and you can return to the same shop hours later for a Subway sandwich at lunch. Big name brands are joining together to share space, double their foot traffic, and lower joint costs. Now that is big thinking. If you have a business of any kind, start brainstorming about someone you can link up with to accomplish these same bottom-line results. Take action.

When you vow to think big in affirmations, think big in visualizations, and think big in action, all three roll over into one big jackpot!

MUCH ABUNDANCE VERSUS SIMPLE ABUNDANCE

Why think big so relentlessly? Because negative outside forces are always there influencing your thoughts, battling for prominence, and all too often diminishing your thinking and killing your dreams. Over and over throughout our lives we hear folks say, "You want do what? That will never happen!"

You need to be on guard and consciously combat small goals and small thinking. Despite extraordinary changes in women's lives over the past 30 years, and despite the facts that some eight million women now operate their own businesses in the United States and that women now comprise 50 percent of the workforce, current widespread media messages are advocating *downscaling* or *simplifying* one's lifestyle. Women are embracing these messages without fully examining the hidden message —once again women are being told (albeit in a warm and fuzzy way) that they should settle for less than what they deserve, and they shouldn't try so hard lest they be disappointed. In the same way that young girls are seldom encouraged in math or sports, women are just not encouraged to think big when it comes to money or success.

No woman who wants to become a millionairess can afford this downscaling attitude! Instead, think of your life as being filled with much abundance, rather than simple abundance!

Think big now in order to feel better about wanting more, rather than trying to learn how to be satisfied with less!

Think big now means that the ranks of America's millionaires are open to all women, regardless of age, education, talent, race, debt, or cash on-hand! The day you picked this book up and started reading is *now.* Waiting until tomorrow, next week, or your next paycheck on the first of the month merely postpones what you want today—millionaire money! Whatever fortune-making idea you have in mind, be it a product, investment, or service, apply your *think big now* philosophy and launch it! Remember, money-making ideas manifest themselves only when you think big, and act on them now with passion, conviction, and self-trust.

Your timing couldn't be better. "Money, money, and more money" is the mantra of the new century. The economy is so robust and so many huge new fortunes exist that *Forbes* magazine revised their standards for inclusion on the annual list of America's wealthiest folks. We are living in an age of *instant-aires,* when fortunes are built overnight and anything is possible.

You can learn to think big now by surrounding yourself with the stories of large sums of money, by studying the people who are already reaping the benefits of thinking big, by listening constantly to money talk, and by digging for your golden inspiration every chance you get.

THINK AND BUILD FOR THE LONG-TERM PAYOFF

Your *think big now* motto must be your watchword today and tomorrow. Working hard and smart, and building as you go, results in a long-term payoff.

Sometimes people *think big* about things that come in small packages. Take, for example, Barbie®—the global icon of dolldom. Her creator Ruth Handler, simply wanted to design a doll that would fit into her five-year-old daughter's tiny hand.

The rest, as they say, is history. In fact, Barbie herself is part of the personal history of many baby boomers. There's almost as much written about Barbie as there is about Princess Diana.

According to Mattel's Jill Barad, the first female president and CEO of Mattel (whose total compensation, by the way, is $6.17 million), Barbie will have her own flagship store in Beverly Hills, go into publishing, and hit the Internet. Already a $5 billion baby, Barbie shows no sign of fading into the sunset.

Here's another doll story. *The Wall Street Journal* reported an incredible 12-year payoff earned by Pleasant Rowland, the creator of American Girl dolls. Back in 1986, Ms. Rowland, a former teacher and reporter, had a young niece. Ms. Roland was frustrated that bombshell Barbie was the toy of choice for young girls, and set out to create an alternative to the plastic princess. She got busy and founded the American Girl doll and book collections. The lines are carefully crafted to give girls seven and older an understanding of American history while fostering pride in the traditions of growing up female in America.

In 1998, *The Wall Street Journal* reported, "Toy giant Mattel, Inc., said it will pay $700 million for closely held Pleasant Company." $700 million! How's that for a payoff? And there's more. Pleasant will head her *autonomous unit* from her hometown of Middleton, Wisconsin, and is slated to become a vice-president of Mattel.

Here's an interesting point to remember: Barbie sells for approximately $15, the American Girl Samantha, $82, but both dolls made their owners millionairesses!

Another role-model millionairess, whose long-term payoff will surely ride into the next century, is mail order queen Lillian Vernon. Despite a lack of formal training, Vernon turned $2,000 in wedding money into a successful mail order business serving 18 million customers.

It's been 45 years since Lillian Vernon's first advertisement appeared in *Seventeen*. "Be first to sport the personalized look on your bag and belt," read the ad, touting a $2.99 leather purse and $1.99 belt. That $495 ad placed by a suburban New York housewife garnered $32,000 worth of orders and launched a mail order empire that finished the 1998 fiscal year with $258.2 million in sales.

A few years ago Vernon received 120,000 orders for the lace Christmas tree angel she designed! "I make quick decisions based on my golden gut instinct," she's been known to say often. Vernon, the queen of free personalization on most merchandise, offers this advice: "Risk your own money, trust your creative instincts, and find someone who can execute your vision."

It's not all smooth sailing, she hastens to add. "Acknowledge and correct your mistakes. You have so many decisions to make, you can't look back." She admits, "To this day I don't know how to read a financial statement. I need help with the numbers."

Not everyone needs help with numbers, though. Certainly not Muriel Seibert, the first woman to buy a seat on the New York Stock Exchange. She was thinking big when she spent $445,000 for the seat in 1967 while everyone around her was thinking she should go home! A trailblazer since she hit Wall Street, "Mickie" is president of the discount brokerage Muriel Seibert & Company.

The 23 lessons in this book are designed to open your eyes and change your thinking about money and success. They have been developed through observation, discussion, and interviews with millionaire women who think big! Women who were not satisfied with what ordinary life seemed to offer and went out and did it all themselves, accomplishing extraordinary business feats and acquiring impressive fortunes along the way. By reading what these women have accomplished, you too will begin to develop a greater sense of what is possible in your life—both financially and personally. So hang on, this is going to be a fast ride through millionairess-land!

EXERCISES

1. Read and take notes from at least five business publications each month, such as *Forbes, Fortune, Entrepreneur, Inc., Nation's Business, Success, The Economist, Money, Black Enterprise,* and *Hispanic Business.* The enormous financial dealings described in *Variety* will especially invigorate your perceptions about money.

2. Make it a habit to read the business section of your local newspaper, as well as *USA Today, The Wall Street Journal, New York Times, San Francisco Chronicle, Los Angeles Times,* and papers from other cities where business trends start.

3. Watch television shows like *Money Report* and *Wall Street Week,* and the financial news on CNN and CNBC. Ditto for radio.

4. Still don't feel connected to all that big money? Call your local chamber of commerce or local business newspaper and ask for a copy of their list of the 25 largest women-owned businesses in your area. Take a look at their annual revenues. If they can do it, so can you.

The point of all this reading and listening is to become more at ease with the large sums of money that fill these stories on a daily basis. These folks, these businesses, made it big by thinking big. Isn't it time you started, too?

5. Now that you are aware of the kind of big money that is floating around you every day, design your own powerful affirmation. Choose the biggest money number you

desire, the largest and most outrageous business goal you have—state the size of your future investment port- folio! Write it out and post it on your mirror, hold it in your heart, repeat it to yourself 25 times a day. "As woman thinketh, so shall she be. As a woman thinketh and doeth so shall she be!"

Know and Believe You Deserve to Be Wealthy

It will be interesting to see how you respond to *The Millionairess Across the Street* because how women respond, relate, think, and act where money is concerned is mighty personal and generally charged with emotion. Will you, for example, see the good and the merit in these millionairesses' money? Or will you have a too-much-money anxiety attack? Maybe you'll fall somewhere in between? The subject of money is not a comfortable one for most women and that's the reason for this lesson.

Our attitudes, beliefs, and interest surrounding money stem from our childhood. The arenas of culture, family, school, religion, politics, law enforcement, and especially the media influence our notions and feelings about money. From a very early age, the mere mention of the word money puts some women on guard. They feel fear, guilt, embarrassment, defensiveness, jealousy, even anger. Often, and because of money, women are forced to lie, cover up, pretend, and make sacrifices. Where and how did we learn these self-defeating behaviors? From our individual environments, of course.

Money, too, has gotten a bad rap. A slew of phrases come to mind: money is the root of all evil, money corrupts, money causes problems (obscene wealth, greedy capitalists), money is power, good money, dirty money, clean money, drug money, blood money—the list goes on and on. Yet a critical point remains: Money is simply a tool. More importantly, practically everything women want and need for themselves and their families—from a reliable car to a comfortable home and good health care—is supplied by money. This why you should *know and believe you deserve to be wealthy,* and why money should be way up there alongside love, health, family, and religion.

One woman who has broken all money records and shares the *know-and-believe-you-deserve-to-be-wealthy* philosophy is Mary Kay Ash of Mary Kay Costmetics. Mary Kay's personal doctrine has always been: "God first, family second, career third." She attributes her success to her initial decision to "take God as our partner," a decision that helps her company attract "spiritually strong people" who promote her cosmetics in 25 countries with missionary fervor.

With Mary Kay there is no false modesty either. When she preaches equal pay for equal work she follows through by rewarding her top saleswomen with diamond-studded pins in the shape of dollar signs, red Grand Ams, and pink Cadillacs—at one time her signature. Her company estimates that more women have earned more than $1 million working for Mary Kay than any other company. In 1995, her mix of faith and facials approached $2 billion at the retail sales level. Incredible! All this from a woman who started her company with her total life savings of $5,000, while supporting three children as a single mother.

Mary Kay Ash is a firm believer in prosperity. She is known for giving her consultants autographed dollar bills with *Matthew 25:14-30* written on them. This scripture is interpreted as "When we do, we shall be given more."

Know and believe you deserve to be wealthy is a deep and necessary credo for women everywhere. It is of vital importance in the courtroom, where the income of divorced women plummets to 70 percent. Why the subject of divorce in a book about millionairesses? According to well-known statistics, one out of two marriages will end in divorce. Divorce can happen to anyone—from stay-at-home wives to business partners and unpaid corporate wives—it has no class boundaries.

Take the case of Lorna Wendt. When her 32-year marriage to GE Capital CEO Gary Wendt ended, she fought for recognition of the value of a corporate wife. Lorna, who dedicated herself to her spouse's career and her family, insisted on being recognized as a full partner. "I complemented him [husband] by keeping the home fires burning and by raising a family and by being the CEO of the Wendt home corporation and by running the household and grounds and social and emotional ties so he could go out and work very hard at what he was good at," she told *Fortune*. "If marriage isn't a partnership between equals, then why get married? If you knew that some husband or judge down the road was going to say, 'You're 30 percent part of this marriage, and he's a 70 percent part,' would you get married?"

Lorna came out of the Connecticut Superior Court with $20 million—far less than the $50 million she sought, but far more than the $8 million her husband had offered.

Lorna actually got more—her own career. By encouraging more women to speak up, she started a full-fledged movement that is raising women's awareness of equitable compensation. Lorna began the Foundation for Equality in Marriage and by its first board meeting it received 1,000 e-mails.

The opposite of a high-asset divorce case is a low-asset one. In the divorce of one woman who was unassertive and non-skilled, the outcome was instant poverty—$300 in child support for three children. Then the patriarchal system shoved her down even more when the judge awarded her car, which was in her name and given to her by her mother, to her spouse!

A different spin on the merit of having and deserving wealth begins with the tale of the multimillionaire secretary Gladys Holm. Although she never earned more than $15,000 annually, she left $18 million to a children's hospital in Chicago when she died. Her secret: Invest a little every month in the stocks her boss was buying. Over the decades, the magic of compounding returns and good stock picks made her a wealthy woman.

A POLITICIAN'S AMERICAN DREAM

Holm's story inspired Senator Bob Kerrey of Nebraska to propose the idea of giving millions of Americans with few assets a similar chance at wealth and security. First, Kerrey would cut employees' share of today's payroll tax by 2 percentage points and put that money into personal accounts that individuals would be forced to invest for their retirement. He would spend another chunk of money—$4 billion, or less than 1 percent of the revenue the payroll tax collects—to open similar $1,000 investment accounts for each of the 4 million babies born in the United States every year. This money would be saved for the children's retirement. Finally, Kerrey would extend the recently enacted $500-per-child tax credit to the parents of 20 million poorer kids who don't currently receive the credit through the bipartisan budget bill. The money would then have to be placed in each child's investment account and couldn't be touched for five years. Kerrey would pay for most of this—and keep Social Security solvent—by lowering beneficiary's annual cost-of-living increases and phasing in higher retirement ages indexed to increases in life expectancy.

Nest eggs. Over time, the impact could be astounding. Assuming that Kerrey's investment accounts produced average yearly returns of 8.5 percent, almost every American born today would accumulate over $1 million by the time he or she turned 65! Today's younger workers would build hefty nest eggs as well.

Others in politics have conceptualized similar theories, but Kerrey has come up with a plan that could actually work. He wants to create wealth—*endowing the future*—instead of just imposing eat-your-spinach austerity. Indeed, *know and believe you and your children deserve to be wealthy!*

If you're the type that needs a cause to enjoy profits then check out these Microsoft millionairesses:

- Ida Cole, 43. After only six years at Microsoft she retired. In June 1993, the Paramount—a gorgeous Beaux Arts-style theater built in 1928—was about to be sacrificed to an expansion of Seattle's convention center. Rallying both old and new money, Cole raised $35 million to purchase and restore the theater.
- Trish Millines, 40. She retired in 1996 with "enough money to live comfortably," and founded Technology Access Foundation with social worker Jill Hull. Their foundation introduces low-income kids to cyberspace. "This is the best job I've ever had," she says of her position as the foundation's executive director. "I love it."

"I love it" is an expression we women use a lot.

Bettina: In all the research books and documents I compiled while writing this book, I kept looking for this exclamation about money. I found only two. The first "I love money. I love its potential to move things ahead, to free the human spirit," says New York Women's Foundation (NYWF) philanthropist Helen Hunt of New York City. The only other reference was by . . . me! From my own book Chiquita's Cocoon: *"I love money! I am very bold about it. With money I feed my children, pro-*

vide for their health needs, educate them and get them out of trouble. I can run my car, make the house payments and take a vacation. Without money life is pretty dull: no books, magazines or videos, no lunches, no clothes, no cosmetics or nice perfumes, no conferences, no traveling, no entertainment and no future plans. When I'm broke, I feel ill and depressed, spiritless and stuck." We have to claim that phrase!

Let's be truthful. To be without money is to suffer. No one says it better than Unity minister Catherine C. Ponder in *The Dynamic Laws of Prosperity:*

> Poverty fills prisons with thieves and murderers. Poverty drives men and women to the vices of alcohol, drugs, prostitution and even suicide. It drives potentially fine, talented children to delinquency and crime. It causes worry, strain and tension, which lead to poor physical and mental health. To live in poverty is to live in a depressed state, a bona fide sickness often undetected and accepted as a normal way to live.

Know and believe you deserve to be wealthy.

EXERCISES

One way to overcome any reservations about money is to discuss them. Next time you are with women friends, don't discuss men, kids, cooking, or shopping. Instead, introduce one of these topics:

- *In childhood:* How much money did your family have or not have, and who controlled it? How money was discussed, secretly or openly, directly affects your money thinking as an adult.

- *In marriage:* Traditionally, marriage is the sanctuary of protection for women, yet husbands and wives rank money first on their list of serious interpersonal problems.
- *In divorce:* "Ninety percent of all divorces are caused by money," according to financial planner and psychologist Victoria Felton-Collins. Economically, women and children suffer severely.
- *In college:* Why do women, unsure of their talent or potential, pursue liberal arts degrees when a math, engineering, or accounting degree would earn them so much more?
- *In the workforce:* How many jobs, at minimum wage, do women still fill? Pay for women appears to be improving mainly because men's pay is going down.
- *In careers:* The famous glass ceiling is being challenged more and more but what is it going to take to shatter it once and for all?
- *In society:* Why is it so difficult for us to socialize with people whose economic status is higher than ours?
- *In religion:* Churches are growing dependent on women's offerings (tithing). What about the stained glass ceiling?

Now take this short *Money and You* quiz. You may surprise yourself.

MONEY AND YOU

Here are some questions about money that can help you understand how money motivates you. They will help you understand how other people view money. You can begin to do a better job working out differences about money with other people. Don't think too long about each question. Just circle the answer that best fits you.

1. If I won $1,000 in the office pool, I would
   a. go on a weekend vacation.
   b. save it for a rainy day.
   c. invest it in hopes of making more money.
   d. buy a gift for someone.

2. If I had more money, I
   a. could do more of what I want to do.
   b. would have fewer problems.
   c. would drive a more expensive car.
   d. could make the lives of those I care about easier.

3. To save money, I
   a. do it when it feels right.
   b. pay myself first every month.
   c. look for high-risk/high-return investments.
   d. plan to save a specific amount each month, but alter my plans if my family needs it.

4. When it comes to discussing my finances, I
   a. don't.
   b. share information when it's valuable to others.
   c. like to tell people how well I'm doing financially.
   d. seek the advice of others often.

5. Before I buy an expensive item, I
   a. make sure I feel good about the purchase.
   b. read consumer magazines.
   c. ask myself, "How will this purchase empower my life?"
   d. seek the opinions of others, particularly friends and family.

6. If I were to come across extra money in my old coat pocket, I would
   a. buy myself something I want.
   b. save the money.
   c. invest the money.
   d. take a friend to lunch.

7. If I buy a generic brand item, I
   a. feel I deserve better, but can't afford better.
   b. feel I'm a smarter shopper.
   c. remove the label so others won't know it's generic.
   d. worry it might not taste right or work right.

8. Keeping up with bills
   a. is not a high priority.
   b. and paying them on time is important.
   c. is assigned to someone else.
   d. is important so people aren't upset with me.

9. Borrowing money
   a. is against my principals.
   b. should be an option when needed.
   c. is valuable for investments and business deals.
   d. from friends and family works best for me.

10. When paying for dinner, I
    a. want people to contribute what they owe me without any hassle.
    b. prefer separate checks.
    c. use my credit card and people can pay me.
    d. like to pay for everyone when I can afford it.

11. Tipping at restaurants
    a. is OK if you get good service.
    b. hurts, but I do it anyway.
    c. should be lavish at fancy restaurants.
    d. is recognition of the hard work that waiters and wait-resses provide.

12. If I won the lottery, I
    a. would quit work and do whatever strikes my fancy.
    b. would continue to work but would enjoy some of the money now.
    c. could expand my business plans tremendously.
    d. would enjoy more time with family and friends.

13. When I can't make up my mind about buying something, I tell myself
    a. to go for it.
    b. it's a great buy.
    c. that a good investment will pay off.
    d. that my friends will enjoy it.

14. In my situation,
    a. I let someone else handle the bills.
    b. I make sure our budget is working.
    c. I make the big financial decisions and my partner is the bargain saver.
    d. my partner and I take turns with financial record-keeping.

MONEY AND YOU ANSWER KEY

Total all a answers, b answers, c answers, and d answers.

_____ a
_____ b
_____ c
_____ d

The letter with the highest number of your responses gives clues about your money motivation: a—freedom, b—security, c—power, or d—kindness.

If most of your answers were a, you use money as a source of freedom. You

- seek independence.
- expect money to provide you with excitement, adventure, new experiences, and new things.
- may buy things for others after you've achieved your desires.
- value the ability to travel and do things more than anything else.
- tend to be either very rich or very poor.
- are a loner when possible.
- have never thought balancing a checkbook or sticking to a budget was something worth doing.

If most of your answers were b, you use money to lay a groundwork of security and safety. You

- crave safety more than anything else.
- value predictability and try to minimize the unknown.
- want stability and know that insurance is valuable to your financial plan.
- stick to well-known, blue chip companies for your investments.
- select low-risk investments.
- stay at the same job for a long time.
- love bargains, coupons, and flea markets.
- balance your checkbook every month.

If most of your answers were c, you know that money buys power. You

- put your energy wholeheartedly into work.
- drive for success.
- like to be in control and are comfortable managing people and projects.
- will strive for the highest position of power possible.
- love competition.
- assign detail to others.
- ignore budgets if they don't fit your plan.
- like to have the newest things first.

If most of your answers were d, you

- spend money to bring pleasure to relationships.
- are thoughtful, kind, caring, and you are always there to help others.
- are your community's best volunteer.
- treat people in special ways and offer them support and nurturing.
- think of money as a way to make life more meaningful to friends and family.

- may sometimes use money to buy love when you're feeling needy.
- may find yourself in conflict between saving money and spending it.

Source: *Couples and Money* by Victoria Felton-Collins. Copyright 1998 by Victoria Felton-Collins. Used by permission of Victoria Felton-Collins, Ph.D., CFP, and partner in Keller, Collins, Hakopian, and Leisure Investment Council, Inc. in Irvine, California. She is the founder of the Investment Strategies Conference for Women, an annual event in Orange County, California. She can be reached at 800-224-7931.

Take Yourself Seriously—Or No One Else Will!

So, now you are committed to *thinking big* as discussed in Lesson 1, and Lesson 2 taught you to *know and believe that you deserve to be wealthy*. What's next? Once you have those two motivational building blocks in place, what else can you put on top of them to keeping building towards wealth? What's next is another lesson over which you have complete control—something you can achieve in an instant. It does not cost money, it does not take years to accomplish. What could it be? This: You must believe in yourself with all your heart and never doubt your ability to achieve your dreams.

You must take yourself seriously. Truly commit to achieving what you have set your mind to and believe that your goals—personal, financial, and family goals—are worthy and you are, without a doubt, capable of achieving them. *Believe in yourself, or no one else will believe in you.*

To achieve big things in life you must have confidence in yourself. Frequently, you also must have the confidence and support of others. But before you can expect other people to have confidence in you and help you achieve your goals, you must be behind *yourself* all the way. If you only commit halfway, you will only achieve half (or less) of what you set out to do.

When you take yourself and your dreams seriously, you can stand up with confidence and announce to the world: "I plan to become a millionairess in the next few years! I plan to ensure that my financial future is one filled with comfort and ease." You can look your friends and family in the eyes and demand their respect for what you plan to achieve. Even if you choose to keep your financial goals and dreams to yourself, you must take them seriously to achieve them.

You also must make certain that you are creating a serious effort to achieve what you desire. Your life and your actions must be fully synchronized. No one will take you seriously if you announce major financial goals but are still seen living an extravagant life. No one will take you seriously if you declare that you plan to be debt-free by the end of the year but are still seen regularly lugging home bags from an expensive department store. And if you can't reign in your own behavior, you won't take yourself seriously either! Your own subconscious will begin to sabotage your efforts with ridicule and self-doubt.

Always keep in mind that your day-to-day actions must match your goals. Stop and think about this throughout the day. "Am I helping myself towards my goals, or did what I just do set me back even farther?" This habit will quickly become ingrained in your mind, and soon you won't have to question it at all. Your life, your behavior, and your goals will all be in synch and moving together.

Want to hear ridicule from your friends and family? Announce that you plan to write a book! Take it from two writers, no one really believes that you can finish. Unless and until they see you hard at work, day after day, pounding out the pages. You too, need to pound out the pages in your own new life, working hard to create the financially free future that you have in mind. It is all too easy to take on the burden of everyone else's doubt and allow it to undermine your self-confidence. Don't let it happen. *Take yourself seriously and soon enough everyone else will too!*

SHUT OUT DOUBT AND DISBELIEF

If you try hard to achieve a big dream for yourself and truly concentrate, you also will be better able to ignore the naysayers in your life. For centuries women have had to shut out the constant doubts and disbeliefs of others in order to achieve big things for themselves.

- *Margaret Thatcher.* A middle-class grocer's daughter raised in a highly class-conscious society, she dreamed that she could someday govern the entire country. Through hard work and a belief in the validity of her dreams, she achieved what she set out to do. After nine years of trying, she was finally elected to Parliament. Never wavering in her belief in herself and her dreams, she climbed the party ranks until she was the head of the Conservative Party. She became England's Prime Minister in 1979 (and Europe's first female elected head of state) and kept the position for much of the eighties. Now Lady Thatcher, she travels the world in luxury, giving lectures to business and political leaders.
- *Debbie Fields.* She had a dream that her chocolate chip cookies could be the basis of a successful retail baking business. She alone believed that it would work. By starting small (in the rented corner of a grocery store) and giving away endless free samples, Debbie Fields built Mrs. Fields, Inc. one chocolate chip cookie at a time. She took her cookie dreams seriously, and so did the investor group who paid $100 million for Mrs. Fields, Inc. in 1994.

- *Doris Drucker.* The wife of famed management guru Peter Drucker, she had spent thousands of hours standing in the back of an auditorium listening to her husband speak. One day she had a brainstorm for an audio device that would help public speakers from the podium. Few who heard her idea took her seriously—she was over 80 and had never been in business before. "My children thought I'd gone off my rocker. Friends were more tactful, but I resented their sometimes patronizing remarks." But Doris Drucker took herself and her ideas very seriously, and soon found a partner who did too. After several years of product development she garnered industry respect as "just another professional customer, not an old lady." She hopes that the product will soon be available for public speakers.

- *Laura Groppe.* An electronic game enthusiast herself, Laura Groppe noticed that most of the games out there were geared towards young boys and men—lots of shoot-'em-up and slash-'em action. What was being developed for young girls to play? Nothing. So Laura took up the task herself. She met with resistance on all sides, hearing over and over that "girls aren't interested in computer games, no matter what the subject." Or, "A company like that couldn't possibly make money." But she took her ideas seriously and continued to try to raise money. Today, her company Girl Games, Inc. runs the popular www.planetgirl.com Web site and has proven that young girls *do* play computer games and a company that caters to them *can* make money!

These women all took themselves seriously. And these women all succeeded.

You must have the self-confidence to believe in yourself, even when others have fallen back and lost confidence in your pursuits. When everyone around you questions your dreams and ridicules your goals, you must have the staying power. Don't look back, don't peer over your shoulder, don't acknowledge the naysayers. Look straight ahead and keep going. You must believe deeply in what you know to be true, regardless of whether anyone else will follow you there.

> *Jennifer: The need to believe in what I know to be true came home for me in a quirky way not long ago. I was driving a stretch of road near my house where the posted speed limit is 55. A sheriff was driving along in one lane at only 40 miles an hour. I came up behind him, thought about it for only a moment, and then passed him in order to continue going 55. In my rear view mirror I could see a whole group of cars behind him, too timid and unsure to pass. Life offered us all 55, but these people seemed willing to accept the sheriff's reality and only go 40. They didn't have the confidence in what they knew to be true to go ahead and claim it.*

Don't be afraid to step up and lay claim to all that life offers you, even if others around you are too frightened to do so. Believe in yourself and the knowledge that you have acquired in life. Don't let others cause you doubt, put your foot on the gas and *go!*

DEVELOP AN AIR OF SUCCESS AND ACHIEVEMENT

Taking yourself seriously will move you a long way towards achieving financial freedom. It also will have a marvelous spill-over effect in the rest of your life—your supreme self-confidence soon will affect the way others look at you. It also will affect the way others treat you. When you begin to take yourself and your plans seriously, you also begin to exude a greater confidence that demands respect. You will have a different air about you, an air of success and achievement. Coworkers, family members, friends, and anyone you come into contact with will soon realize that this is a woman to be reckoned with.

And the best part is, when this wonderful effect starts to kick in it will only reinforce how you feel about yourself! And that will continue to increase the respect that you get from others—it just goes on and on!

If you begin to act as though you have *already* accomplished your goals and achieved your dreams, then you will move much more quickly on the path towards financial success. And don't forget to *look* as though you have already accomplished your goals. No, you don't have to drape yourself in furs, but you must make an effort to dress in a way that commands respect. When you look sharp, you act sharp.

You must also take yourself seriously whenever you are negotiating. Whether it is something as simple as negotiating a better price on a dress that is missing a button, or as complex as negotiating a better price on a car, take yourself and your needs seriously.

"When I first started in the insurance business, it was hard to be taken seriously by the older men in the office. But I just kept at it. I made sure that I knew the facts. I spoke up at meetings, and I let them know that I took myself and my commitment to this business seriously," Rita Gibson told us. And because Rita took herself seriously, it has paid off handsomely. Not only did she succeed and prosper in the insurance business, but she has hit every one of the financial goals she set for herself.

So remember, in your quest for financial success, always *take yourself seriously, or no one else will!*

EXERCISES

Here are five affirmations that you may write out or repeat to yourself on a daily basis. Feel free to create your own affirmations for money and success.

1. I take myself seriously and know that I will achieve everything that I put my mind and my efforts behind.

2. I take myself and my dreams seriously, even when others around me express doubt.

3. I take myself seriously and will work hard to achieve my financial dreams.

4. I take myself seriously and my self-confidence inspires others to trust and believe in me.

5. When I behave as though I have already achieved my goals, I am that much closer to attaining them.

LESSON 4

Discover Your God-Given Passion and Package It!

So many of us have put in our time as punch-the-clock employees, watching our lives slip away as we worked hard on someone else's behalf. No matter how much we claim to enjoy our corporate jobs—the challenges, the teamwork, the paycheck every two weeks—do not overlook the fact that every hour you work is dedicated to making someone wealthy. And that someone isn't you.

Face it, few people ever get rich working for someone else. If you work for a privately owned business, your hard work and efforts are enriching the owners and their families. If you work for a publicly owned company, your hard work and efforts are enriching the company's stockholders. Either way, you are definitely not the person being enriched. As a matter of fact, it may well be in the company's interest to pay you as little as they can! Every dollar they pay to you is one less dollar for the owners or stockholders, so why on earth would they want to pay you a high salary? Think about it!

Do you spend much of your time grousing about how under-paid you are? Take it from us, it is useless to resent it. If you owned the business, would you do it differently? The fact of the matter is, it makes good business sense.

Move away from placing the blame for your sagging financial fortunes on your employers and direct your energy into another category. Instead of focusing on trying to get other people to pay you more, focus on how *you* can use your own talents, energy, creativity, and *passion* to prosper on your own.

TAKE A CHANCE ON YOURSELF

Don't believe us? Here is a vivid case in point. Harriet Rubin was the well-known publisher of Currency Books for Double-day in New York. A few years ago, her net worth was around $200,000. Not bad, but not the big bucks. Unhappy about how her life was proceeding, she took a chance on herself by leaving her job and writing a book herself instead of publishing other people's work—and it paid off handsomely. A scant two years later her net worth is over $1 million all because, for the first time ever, she poured her efforts and creativity into a book project that *she* owned and profited from, not the company she worked for. Way to go, Harriet!

When you put your passion to work for yourself by creating an income for you instead of creating money for your employer, there is no holding back. Your passions, your loves, your interests —any of these might well hold the key to increasing your net worth!

Harriet Rubin's passion was the struggle to succeed as a woman in a man's world, as a woman striving to publish impor-tant business books. She began to look for role models in the strong and courageous women who had triumphed in earlier centuries. It occurred to her that other women might be interested in what she found. Her book *The Princessa*—filled with leadership and strategy secrets for women trying to succeed— became a best-seller. Do you have a passion that millions of other people might be interested in, too?

Speaking of passion, a rather graphic example of packaging passion comes to us from England (not always thought of as a passionate place). Ann Summers is a company that is run by women, sells to women, and employs 7,000 women to sell its products at home parties. What do they sell? Sex toys and fancy lingerie! Jacqueline Gold is the head of the Ann Summers empire, which she runs with the help of an all-women board of directors. The company is now worth $64 million and is among Britain's most profitable public companies. Passion at its finest!

Let's return to less shocking examples of packaging your passion for profit. America's own Martha Stewart is among the best examples of how to create wealth by channeling your own personal passions into a business endeavor, a $150 million a year endeavor. Martha Stewart loved to cook, loved to throw beautiful parties, loved to make beautiful things out of dried flowers and twisted vines. She wondered if perhaps there were other women out there who also might be interested in these things—and her multimedia empire is the result. Some women love her, some women hate her, but all women should hail her as an extraordinary example of entrepreneurial passion and zeal. Talk about "do what you love and the money will follow!" Has it ever!

PASSION IS . . .

We've been throwing the word *passion* around quite a bit in this lesson, but are you clued in to just what we mean? What is a *passion?* A passion is anything that you are . . . well, passionate about! Are you wild about gardening? So are millions of other folks! If you have an idea for a better gardening tool, or a folksy wooden bench to relax on, will there be a market for it? Yes! Are you passionate about food and cooking? So was Martha Stewart, and you know she doesn't make any mistakes!

Michele Hoskins was passionate about food, too. Her passion was for the taste of her great-great-grandmother's famed syrup. Michele took that passion—and that recipe—and sold every one of her possessions to fund the syrup business. Today, Michele Foods of Calumet City, Illinois, pulls in more than $7 million a year. Tasty!

Do you have a passion for design, crafts, or music? You might well be able to develop a viable money-making idea out of it. Years ago Susan Shutz was a young woman who liked to write poetry. She married a young man who liked to paint with watercolors. Determined to find a profitable outlet for their talents, they founded Blue Mountain Press. The poet and the artist now pull in over $1 million from poetry and painting! They publish books and greeting cards featuring poetry penned by Susan, with illustrations painted by her husband Jim.

Imagine the thrill and the emotional and psychological rewards that will come your way if you can devote your energies and passion towards doing something that will benefit *you* instead of someone else. Once you harness your passion and tap into the energy that arises when you are engaged in doing something you enjoy instead of something you endure—the possibilities are endless!

With passion on your side, you will find it easy to jump out of bed even earlier than usual, ready to get to work on something you love—something that benefits *you*. Motivational master Anthony Robbins encourages everyone to harness their passion, "Passion is unbridled power to move our lives forward at a faster tempo than ever before." Grab onto that power and go!

Are passions always related to hobbies or talents? Certainly not, a passion is whatever turns you on, whatever makes your heart race. Audrey Quackenbush of Jacksonville, Florida, discovered her passion by accident. While working as a controller for a chemical company she happened to drive a friend's big truck. She liked the thrill of driving a big rig so much that she became a trucker, too. But she didn't stop at just owning one truck. Her passion for trucks has driven her all the way to the top. Audrey's company, White Line Trucking, pulls in revenues of $5 million a year. Is that something you could feel passionate about?

Not everyone feels passionate about high technology. In fact, some of us feel downright nervous around it. Not Esther Dyson, though, she has built her passion for the world of high tech into a successful newsletter and conference business. Her New York company, EDventure Holdings, not only puts on the annual PC Forum conference, but also has branched out to include a venture-capital fund to invest in emerging markets and an international conference on high technology. Does anyone else recognize Esther's passion? Yes, last year a book publisher paid Esther a cool $1 million to write a book in which she shares her passion for PCs with ordinary readers.

What else can inspire passion? "I live and breathe this business," says Jo Malone about the business she developed called Jo Malone. What kind of a business does she live and breathe? Perfume! Jo was passionate about the way things smelled, and turned her passion into a $2 million a year line of perfumed colognes, soaps, and lotions.

MAKE PASSION WORK FOR YOU

Okay, you're thinking, how wonderful that these lucky women have been able to turn their passions into big chunks of cash. But what about me? I don't feel passionate about anything right now. I'm so worn out by the time I get home at night that

I don't have an extra minute to think about anything other than how I am going to get up again tomorrow morning.

And what if you aren't in the least bit interested in starting your own business? All we have been saying for the past few pages seems to apply only to women who are ready to quit their jobs and start up businesses about which they can be passionate. How can you make passion work for you then? Despite our little lecture at the beginning of this lesson—that as an employee your efforts are all channeled towards making money for someone else—you still can harness what Anthony Robbins called that *unbridled power* or passion.

You still can use passion to turn up the volume in your life, to energize you, and to help you stay focused on your money goals. You can become passionate about paying down debt, acquiring a nest egg, or saving money. Whatever it is you do—go *all* the way!

You can discover your God-given passion for the best that life has to offer!

- A passion for living
- A passion for money
- A passion for accumulating wealth

Passion comes from within. Passion comes from allowing yourself to fall in love with something—from the feeling you get when you do something creative, to the satisfaction that you feel when you are proud of the work you do. Passion will give you the energy to persevere.

"If someone had told me years ago that I would someday be working in commercial real estate, I would have said 'What is that?'" Bonnie Marx told us. "But yet, here I am and I love what I am doing. You really can learn to love something. Life is a journey, you will come across things that interest you every day. As you start to gather knowledge and information about those new things that interest you, you will start to turn those interests into new skills."

What does Bonnie mean? That you might not have a marketable passion today, but tomorrow you might pick up the newspaper, or pass by a sign on the road, and something will prick your interest. And a new passion will arise, just like that!

EXERCISES

Sometimes our passions really are hard to discover. It may seem like such an ordinary part of your life—the fact that you love reading or that you enjoy helping friends plan their vacations—that you easily can overlook something that you are truly passionate about. So let's look around your life.

1. Clear the decks, mentally. Concentrate on the word *passion*. What do you see? Imagine a passionate life, one in which you spring out of bed every morning. What do you see your life revolving around? Write down some of those images.

2. Try the word *excitement*. What excites you? What thrills you? Jot these things down.

3. Don't imprison your passion, practice it! Practice showing your passion with your voice, your body language, and in all your communications.

4. When boredom, exhaustion, or small failures lure you away from your goals, rekindle your passion with a brisk walk, workout, or even a good passion-pinch.

5. Passion indicates belief and conviction, so another way to find your passion is to ask yourself "What do I believe in? Where do my convictions lie?"

6. Stop thinking about just yourself, because your passion for life may very well be doing for others. It's worth a thought or two.

LESSON 5

Create Your Own Brain Trust or Mastermind

In order to truly succeed in life, both on a financial and personal level, you need to be surrounded by people who can support you in your efforts. A group of people who themselves have high standards of excellence and are committed to attaining incredible personal goals. A group of people who can give advice, encouragement, emotional support, and perhaps a warm hug if needed.

Doesn't this sound wonderful? Who are these terrific people, and where can you find them? Are they free for lunch tomorrow?

This incredible group of people is called a *mastermind* or a *brain trust*. And because everyone needs different sorts of people in their mastermind, it is a group that you will have to build on your own.

What is a mastermind? What is in a brain trust? A mastermind or brain trust is a collection of successful people that you gather around you intentionally, for the sole purpose of helping you to achieve great things and continue to be inspired towards reaching your goals.

In the classic motivational book *Think and Grow Rich,* Napoleon Hill defined a mastermind as, "coordination of knowledge and effort, in the spirit of harmony, between two or more people for the attainment of a definite purpose." Gee, it sure sounds like a fun group. But the world has changed greatly since Hill first wrote his book in the twenties, and the ideas behind mastermind groups have changed along with it. As examples of mastermind groups, Hill cites the people that Andrew Carnegie and Henry Ford surrounded themselves with. Carnegie in particular attributed much of his incredible financial achievement (he was ultimately one of the world's richest men, having built a fortune in the steel business) to his mastermind group.

An example more current than the steel industry at the turn of the century can be found in the troika of David Geffen, Stephen Speilberg, and Jeffrey Katzenberg, the founders of DreamWorks SKG. Three talented men who consulted each other regularly when they were each in different businesses—for advice, encouragement, and shared knowledge. They found that their combined knowledge and creativity helped them do extraordinary things, things that they might not have been able to do without the encouragement of the others. And when they realized that their talents and knowledge would be more powerful if they pooled them, the DreamWorks studio was formed.

Not every mastermind group starts a business together, mind you. And although we think masterminds should be groups of three or more, you also can see the same dynamic in the friendship of Bill Gates of Microsoft and Warren Buffett of Berkshire Hathaway. Two of the world's richest men, they have formed a unique and close friendship in the last few years. While Buffett professes not to really understand most of the high-tech world, just think what these two must talk about in private. Aside from their mutual affection for a Coke-and-hamburger diet, just think how much more brain power and creativity exists when the two of them are in the room together? Awesome.

PUT TWO MINDS TOGETHER

What can a mastermind or brain trust help you achieve? And because you formed it, are you the only one who will benefit from this group? Seems like an awfully selfish and greedy motive on which to pull together a group of people.

One mind, no matter how brilliant and creative, can only achieve so much. Two minds put together can double that output. But by grouping together three or four minds, hearts, and creative spirits, the possibilities and brain power are unstoppable! No, you will not be the only one to benefit from this group. By collecting a group of people with the intention of sharing everyone's collective intelligence, all members of a mastermind will benefit. Everyone's potential is multiplied many times over as a result of the group getting together.

Motivational master Mark Victor Hansen formed a mastermind in which every member is a millionaire many times over. Imagine the extraordinary group that must be! Mark regularly credits his mastermind group with having made a huge difference in his life and his achievements. If your goal is to become a millionairess, should you try to put together a group strictly on the basis of income? Not necessarily. You need to surround yourself with financially like-minded people whose goals are in synch with yours. You need to link up with people who have *already* achieved some (if not all) of the things you plan to achieve. Business people, creative people, positive and upbeat influences can help you stay on target on a daily, weekly, monthly, and yearly basis.

Is *mastermind* just a fancy name for that old career standby, *networking?* Or perhaps just *mentoring* in disguise? No. Both networking and mentoring are focused strictly on career advancement, not on enhancing one's life and achieving great personal and financial goals. Networking generally focuses on finding a better job, or a new client, or a new professional contact. It is focused on a one-time interaction. You make your new contact and then move on. Mentoring is a longer process, but once again, it is mainly focused on career advancement. Mentors are skilled old hands who take a young pup under their benevolent wings, promising to help nurture and shape the fledgling's career (generally shaping it into something exactly like their own career). Remember, a mastermind is a whole group of people.

> *Jennifer: When I started my own company after working for many years as an employee, I knew that one of my biggest problems would be battling loneliness and keeping my energy and motivation high. After working in a large company with a constant flow of people around, it really is hard to suddenly be at home, just you and a humming computer. I knew that in order to stay on target with my goals I would need to surround myself with a group of people who had already done what I was trying to do—build a solo career in the publishing field. I called everyone whose work I admired and invited them to a "working dinner party." I told them that I was forming a brain trust, the Book Business Brain Trust, and I believed they had something to contribute to that brain trust. Most were flattered, and agreed to attend. That was the start of an incredibly motivating group that has benefited all six people who belong. We talk over business and personal challenges, brainstorm solutions, and keep everyone on target to achieve their goals. I couldn't do without it!*

If your goal is to become a millionairess, should you limit yourself to only seeking out other women for your mastermind group? Heavens no! Cast a wide net and try to bring as many energetic and energizing men and women as you can. Don't limit yourself when it comes to reaching out and asking others to help you in your quest.

FORM YOUR OWN MASTERMIND—TODAY

How do you go about forming a mastermind? Just like Jennifer and the Book Business Brain Trust, you will have to take the first steps towards organizing one on your own. You will have to work up the nerve to call the people you admire and invite them. A scary idea, but something that you must do.

The best way to bring people together is to suggest a casual lunch or breakfast meeting. Choose a suitable location—a restaurant or café that is pleasing to the eye and will put your fellow masterminders at ease—not a crummy dive in a dicey part of town. And yes, you will probably have to foot the bill for that meeting! Don't forget, at this early stage you are inviting people (some of whom you might not know well) to join you in something that is new to them. Soon they will understand that they, too, can benefit from being a part of a mastermind group. But attending that first meeting might be just as scary to them as it is to you while trying to arrange it!

What if you want to approach people who intimidate you? What if the ideal member for your mastermind group is one of the biggest, richest, and most important people in town? Why on earth would they be willing to help? Here are a few reasons (which might surprise you!).

- It is flattering to be asked to join a mastermind group. You are telling this person, "I admire you and your success, and I believe that I can learn from you."

- Many successful people feel they owe a debt and should help others to succeed because early on someone helped *them!*
- It can be quite gratifying to watch someone else succeed and know that you had a hand in it.

Once you are successful in gathering together a mastermind or brain trust group, will you forever have to organize meetings and pay for lots of lunches and dinners? No. As a matter of fact, your mastermind group doesn't even have to meet in person. Phone conferences are easy and can be just as inspiring and encouraging for all involved. The idea of a phone-based mastermind—or even an e-mail one!—might be even more appealing to busy folks.

EXERCISES

1. Draw up a list of your dream mastermind group. Don't let your fears hold you back in this exercise—dream big. Would you want to have a mastermind with Lillian Vernon, Mary Kay Ash, and Oprah Winfrey to encourage you towards your goals? Write it down! Look around your own town, too. Who are the biggest and most successful people?

2. Set goals and timelines for establishing a mastermind group. Set a firm date for when you'd like to have a mastermind group up and running. Start immediately gathering these people so you can complete your task on time!

3. Affirmations to help you on your way:

- I am surrounding myself with a mastermind of successful and prosperous people.

- I am benefiting from the wisdom, encouragement, and advice of my mastermind.

- Many minds together can accomplish what one mind cannot.

4. If you are still a bit timid about trying to form a real mastermind, why not form an imaginary one? Start to read the biographies of historical figures that you admire, or even successful contemporary figures. Learn what you can from the books, but also hold imaginary meetings with them. Imagine the kind of advice they would give you, and picture them encouraging you to reach for higher goals and achievements.

Employ
Butt-Breaking
Behavior

There's the first shift, the second shift, and now the third shift—and women are conquering them all. The first shift refers to the 60 million women who make up the 9-to-5 workforce that today is like a nonstop rising empire. The second shift commits these same women to domestic duty from dinner time to bedtime. It's the new third shift, however, that has women like Sheree Mitchell employing butt-breaking behavior.

Sheree Mitchell of Columbus, Georgia, used to be a pediatric nurse. Now her former hospital colleagues sometimes ask, "How's your little day care doing?" Her *little* day care center, Growing Room, Inc. which she started nine years ago, has more than 100 employees, occupies more than 27,000 square feet in two child development centers, and expects to bring in more than $2.3 million this year. But, says Mitchell, "Being a woman business owner really is a 24-hour-a-day job."

Just what do we mean by *butt-breaking behavior?* We mean constant hard work, being persistently relentless in pursuit of your goals, employing imaginative problem solving to overcome any obstacles in your way. The sad truth is, nobody ever got wealthy sitting on the couch watching Oprah (but you sure made her a rich woman!). You need to kick your energy into high gear in order to achieve big things!

Jack Canfield, one of the authors of the *Chicken Soup for the Soul* series, likes to tell writers about his butt-breaking behavior and the critical role it played in selling more than 30 million copies of the books. Blow by blow he outlines the steps that he and Mark Victor Hansen took to make their books massive bestsellers. Jack's wife overheard another writer in the audience say, "I'd never do all that work." Mrs. Canfield touched the man on the shoulder and said, "And that's why you won't ever be a best-selling author." Touché!

THE THIRD SHIFT

For Bonnie Williamson, former teacher, self-publisher, and author of seven books, the third shift would begin way before dawn. "I'd write from 4:00 AM to 6:00 AM, dress for work, leave the house at 7:00 AM, drop off a chapter or two at my editor's house, and arrive at work by 8:00. Many times though, I'd get to my editor's by 6:00 AM, squeeze in a 45-minute joint session, then head for work. After school, I'd swing by my editor's house again to pick up the morning's work, go home, correct papers, fill book orders, fix dinner, chat with my husband and go to bed nine-ish. I did these 20-hour days for years," says Bonnie, now retired and living well off her books, especially her recently revised bestseller, *A First-Year Teacher's Guidebook.*

Working hard for money has its rewards but would you do butt-breaking work for free? Lisa Renshaw of Baltimore did. At 21, with only a high-school education and fantasies of owning her own business, Lisa volunteered to work *free* for three months for the owner of a failing parking garage. Her hope: If she could turn the business around he might make her a partner. Instead, after she secured a $3,000 loan so he could pay the rent, he disappeared with the cash.

In a real bind, Renshaw negotiated a lower rent. Because she could only afford one employee, she often worked the 5:30 AM to 1:30 PM shift, parking the cars herself and even washing them (a unique service she thought of). The remaining part of the afternoon she spent on A-to-Z business matters. Because she couldn't spare commuting time, she chased the rats out of a back room in the unheated garage, rolled out of a piece of carpet on the floor, and moved in.

And her business soared.

But three-and-half years later, she was still sleeping in the garage because expenses (especially liability insurance) were way too high. To spread costs, she borrowed $3,500 from her father to use as a down payment on a nearby lot and, with income from two garages, was eventually able to acquire a third. By the time she turned 32, Renshaw headed a multimillion dollar empire with nine locations in Baltimore, directed a staff of 125, and was living in a fashionable part of town. Now, 30-something, Renshaw controls 51 garages in Maryland, Washington, D.C., and Virginia, with $25 million in revenues.

As you can see, the thing about having to employ butt-breaking behavior is that it really never ends until you get to where you want to be, and it seldom ends even then. And unless you're one of the lucky ones, you'll pretty much find yourself going at it alone because one of the biggest challenges still facing women who want to grow a business is the conflict between work and family. Like mail order queen and millionairess Lillian Vernon (who at 69 still works 9 to 5 and is out businessing-it almost every night of the week) bluntly said in her autobiography, *An Eye for Winners,* "My first husband just wasn't the entrepreneurial type so I divorced him."

TAKE A LOOK AT THESE NUMBERS

Despite the costs, statistics show that more women are putting in that third shift. The National Foundation for Women Business Owners (NFWBO) in Silver Spring, Maryland, reports this phenomenal picture:

- There were nearly 8 million women-owned businesses in the United States as of 1996.
- Women-owned businesses employ 18.5 million people.
- Home-based businesses owned by women employ 14 million people.
- Women entrepreneurs are taking their firms into the global marketplace at the same rate as all U.S. business owners.
- Women-owned firms offer the same basic benefits as other firms and are more likely to offer flextime, tuition reimbursement, and profit sharing.
- Women-owned businesses are as financially sound and creditworthy as the typical firm in the U.S. economy, regardless of industry or firm size.
- Women-owned firms are more likely to remain in business than the average U.S. firm. Nearly ¾ of women-owned firms were in business three years later, compared to ⅔ of all U.S. firms.
- Women business owners have different styles of success than their male counterparts. Women value relationships as well as factual information, and are more likely to seek out the opinions of others.

Just who and what kind of women make up this incredible force? Well, some will sound very familiar to you. According to *Working Woman* (1997), as cited in *Hoover's Handbook of American Business,* America's top 20 women business owners include:

Rank	Owner	Company	1997 Revenues Sales in Millions
1	Martha Ingram	Ingram Industries	$11,500
2	Loida Nicholas Lewis	TLC Beatrice	2,230
3	Marian Ilitch	Little Caesar Enterprises	1,800
4	Maggie Hardy Magerko	84 Lumber	1,500
5	Lynda Resnick	Roll International	1,450
6	Antonia Axson Johnson	Axel Johnson Group	1,300
7	Linda Wachner	Warnaco Group	1,060
8	Liz Minyard and Gretchen Minyard Williams	Minyard Food Stores	923
9	Gay Love	Printpack	805
10	Donna Karan	Donna Karan International	613
11	Ardath Rodale	Rodale Press	500
12	Christine Liang	ASI Asia Source Inc.	468
13	Donna Wolf Steigerwaldt	Jockey International	450
14	Helen Copley	The Copley Press	421
15	Jenny Craig	Jenny Craig	401
16	Irma Elder	Troy Motors	381
17	Patricia Gallup	PC Connection	350
18	Barbara Levy Kipper	Chas. Levy Company	350
19	Jane O'Dell	Westfall-O'Dell Transportation Service	350
20	Ellen Gordon	Tootsie Roll Industries	341

This list of successful women business owners goes on:

- Jessica McClintock owns 100 percent of her women's clothing manufacturing company whose revenues last year totaled $145 million.
- Margot Fraser owns 100 percent of Birkenstock Footspring Sandals, Inc. with annual revenues of $55 million.
- Ana Tokunaga, Josie Jurczenia, and Ginny Holmes own 100 percent of Sweet Potatoes, Inc., a children's clothing manufacturer, which pulled in $13 million last year and is still growing.

And imagine how hard they had to work in order to achieve those knock-out numbers—butt-breaking behavior!

One of our favorite stories, which ran in *Entrepreneur,* is about Dineh Mohajer, who as a 22-year-old University of Southern California premed student really went through the challenge of butt-breaking behavior. It all began in the summer of '95, when Dineh was envisioning a summer of partying and kicking back with her boyfriend. Instead, she got something else. One day she went shopping wearing a shade of baby blue nail polish she had mixed herself. A saleswoman at Charles David, an upscale boutique in Santa Monica, California, begged Dineh to reveal her source because the polish complemented Charles David's spring line of shoes. Complimented by a whole lot of other folks that day, as well as many before, Dineh and her sister Pooneh decided to "start selling this stuff." Over burgers and fries, they came up with the name Hard Candy, made up some sample bottles of nail polish in sky (pale blue), sunshine (yellow), mint (green), and violet (lavender) and trotted to market. They made prototypes by blending ready-made polish, like dark blue mixed with white, and adding thinner for the right consistency.

"We were talking in Charles David's about how much we would sell it to them for and how much the store would have to sell it for, and then this girl who was like 16 came running over and said, 'Oh my god, I love these! I have to buy these. How much are they?' We didn't know, but suddenly the sales-woman jumps in saying $18 a bottle. The girl's mother's eyeballs practically dropped out of her head, but the daughter was hav-ing a fit and the mother bought them. Four of them cost, like $75. The owner turned to me and said, 'Okay. Bring me 200 more tomorrow.'"

Hard Candy hit hard and fast and big, from the Santa Monica store to *Seventeen, Elle, Vogue,* and then Nordstrom, Blooming-dale's, and Saks.

During those 18 months, "It was just crazy," says Dineh. "At one point we had 12 people working out of a two-room guest house. Every room was polluted with this stuff. Not only was the business physically overwhelming, but it was also a mental chal-lenge of Olympian proportions. I didn't know anything about business. I was overwhelmed and burned out." Nine months after starting the company, Dineh nearly ended up hospitalized from exhaustion.

Even though Dineh's mom came to her daughter's rescue with a lot of moral support, her office expertise, and a six-figure loan, Hard Candy just kept growing and so did Dineh's exhaus-tion. "I didn't sleep. I didn't eat. I was a working fool," Dineh confesses.

Eventually, and near the brink of collapse, Dineh did the smart thing: She hired an experienced cosmetic CEO.

By working her butt off in a hectic, home-based girlish con-cern, Dineh became a serious contender in the competitive world of cosmetics and created a $10 million nail polish com-pany in Beverly Hills, California.

Call it being an entrepreneur, self-employed, or running a home-based business—the path to success requires the same butt-breaking behavior. Your quality of life improves but the stress level generally increases. Not having a steady income until business booms is part of it; loneliness becomes real when you're at work at 10 PM on a Saturday night, week after week, month after month.

So why do women do it? There are lots of positives. You're the boss. You're in control of your own fate. You are more satisfied and more self-actualized because you are putting your talents forward. You no longer have to hassle with office politics, wait for approval on ideas, or deal with long commutes because a phone, fax, and computer can keep you and your business connected. You tend to be more physically active. You'll keep a better home and probably participate more in family activities than you did when working for someone else. In addition, because you are building something you desire and believe in, you will be more optimistic about business and life in general.

BREAKING INTO THE BANK VAULT

The number one problem for women business owners is lack of access to capital. Those four-page application packets take time and energy to fill out. It takes even more time, energy, and persistence to shop them around from one financial institution to another. Yet you gotta do it! Oh, and that application is going to have to be based on a strong business plan, requiring some hard thinking, good research, and lots of polishing. You must be prepared to respond to and defend any and all parts of your business plan. When you don't have perfect credit, you'll need to be able to explain why in a persuasive manner that minimizes the problem—a speech that you'll surely be giving over and over. But don't give up. The more you do it, the more you perfect it. One more thing: Because success is built on relationships, networking with all the new people you meet along your pathway will take, yes, more butt-breaking behavior.

Timewise, what are we talking? Well, there's a joke about getting an SBA (Small Business Administration) loan: By the time you get it, you really deserve it or you don't need it any more. Sheree Mitchell, our $2.3 million star with the day care centers, says the first time she sought an SBA-guaranteed loan, it took her a year to get it. When she went back to get additional financing, it took two weeks. She attributes her success to a strong business plan and "a bank that believed in me and still does." According to the SBA, by the third quarter of 1998 they backed 10,787 loans worth $1.67 billion to women business owners.

Lesson 14 goes into greater detail as to how to get money. For now, suffice it to say, you can find money in oodles of places including family and friends, banks, finance companies, venture capitalists, investors, and even angels. Each, of course, has its own application policy and procedure. Yep, you guessed it, more and more butt-breaking behavior.

When it comes to women breaking barriers, crashing glass ceilings, and becoming millionaires, there's another issue to be aware of and that's employing butt-breaking behavior against discrimination. It's a fact: A working woman still only makes 71 cents to a man's $1. It's not much different at the top. A recent *Newsweek* cover story focused on America's *new rich*. Of the 22 faces that graced the cover photo, only 3 were women's. (And of these three, none was given featured space within the article itself.) Why? A recent investment brochure statistic claims that 43 percent of those with $500,000 or more in investments are women, so why so few women's faces on a magazine about wealth? On the loan-me-money scene you may have to hang-in even tougher. "People have seen women that are very successful in business," says William Young, president and chief executive of American River Bank, a Sacramento-based community bank. "But that attitude isn't universal even today. You have loan officers that are accustomed to looking at a certain kind of borrower. Women borrowers sometimes still don't fit the profile," Young said.

When it comes to gender issues, a lot of women look the other way. Their thinking: This is the '90s and feminist equality was a thing of the '60s. (They can afford to think that way because the path was paved for them by their predecessors.) Yes, we've come a long way, but no woman is exempt from discrimination, regardless of what era she comes from. The financial frontier still challenges us daily. And you need to make sure that your butt-breaking behavior is both recognized and rewarded!

Bettina: My daughter Mari, a 24-year-old account executive and top saleswoman at her agency, was promised a bonus if she worked hard and met all of the projections. But when she did, she was told she wouldn't be getting it after all due to changes in the program. When she went in to the boss and demanded the promised bonus, she was told, "You're so young. You don't need all that money." In another instance, Mari, a butt-breaking and very visionary Generation X-er, created a sure-thing money-making national program. After months of working out all the bugs and making a polished pitch, she let management know "it's my idea, I want to work it alone. I want to reap the benefits—the money." Again management responded, "You're ambitious and have lots of time to make money. Why not share your pie with the others?"

I'm proud to say that my daughter is a fighter. She fought for her bonus and got it. For her butt-breaking sales record she received $2,500 in stocks (which in this company is only reserved for management). As for the gourmet pie idea she cooked up and presented, it's still in the oven. She's watching vigilantly, making sure she doesn't get burned.

Bettina's daughter worked her butt off and didn't back down when she was denied the bonus she'd been promised. Bonnie Williamson worked her butt off on her self-published books and can now live off the proceeds. Lisa Renshaw worked her butt off and now presides over a multimillion dollar parking garage empire. Dineh Mohajer worked her butt off to make Hard Candy a huge success. So, think about it: What can *you* start working towards?

EXERCISES

1. If you don't already have one, run to your nearest book-store and get a book about time management. Better yet, get that book on a cassette or CD you can listen to in the car or while exercising. These programs can help you ex-tend your time tremendously.

2. Talk with family, friends, and neighbors about your new adventure; explain your time-consuming goals. They'll need to understand why you are so unavailable.

3. Practice saying, "No, thank you," to all invitations beck-oning you away from your work.

4. When you need to close your eyes, close them—20 min-utes max.

5. To keep yourself on track and motivated, call a meeting of your mastermind group!

6. Follow this advice from the classic movie *Norma Rae:* When Norma is about to drop, just an inch short of the goal, she's told by her cohort to "work harder and sleep less."

LESSON 7

Goals— Written Goals!

Goals, what a pretty word! It sounds a bit like a cross be-tween *gold,* and *jewels.* And like the gold and jewels that we all lust after, it is a critical element in our future wealth success. As women on the way to accumulating wealth, we need to have a whole treasure chest of goals that we can focus on every day, a treasure chest overflowing with bright and shining goals.

What are goals? Putting aside the sports definitions, the dictio-nary defines a goal as *an objective.* Something which you would like to achieve. Something to which you aspire. An objective that, once achieved, will fill you with the pride of accomplishment and inspire you to go on and attain the next goal on your list, and the next, and the next.

So many motivational books have devoted page after page to the power of written goals. Some of what has been written leans rather heavily towards the mystical side of goal setting—the new age philosophical idea that once a goal is written, all of the mys-tical powers of the universe will then combine to help you achieve it. Even dry and methodical financial books have latched onto the basic idea that, if you write something down on paper, somehow it has a better chance of happening.

Is there really something magical about writing down goals? Does the power of the universe really put its force behind helping you achieve something once you've written it down? Well, sorry, we don't think so. We have a much more clear-eyed view of why writing down goals can help you achieve them—it is like creating a master *to do* list for your life.

When you write down your goals you are stating right there in black and white what you would like to achieve in your life. Exactly the same way you write down your *to do* list of things that need to be accomplished every day at home or at work, everything from picking up the dry cleaning to finishing the marketing report on that big project. Once you see it there on your list and look at it daily, you naturally strive to complete the task so that you can enjoy the sensation of drawing a thick black line through it. And the very same impulse will help you start working to achieve whatever personal goals you choose for yourself—once you put it down on paper, your written goals will start to nag you a bit, to nudge you towards achieving them. "Hmmm," you might think to yourself, "I did write some pretty big things down, I guess I'd better start taking small steps to achieve them. Otherwise, whenever I look at this list, I will feel depressed and overwhelmed. I wouldn't want to disappoint *myself!*" You (not the universe) will begin to take the steps you need to lead you to the point when you can take your pen and draw a thick black line through even your biggest goal—*Achieved!*

An oft-quoted story concerns a study made of a graduating class at Yale University. Upon graduation, the students were polled to see how many had written down goals for the next phase of their lives. Written goals about dream jobs, financial achievements, personal rewards, family life, and other kinds of accomplishments. Three percent of the class admitted they had written their goals down. At a class reunion 20 years later, the same issue was studied. And guess what? Those 3 percent who had written down their goals 20 years before, were found to be the most accomplished alums in their class. They had great careers, political success, family success, and (you guessed it!)—wealth.

Other than Yale grads, what other kinds of people have found that written goals have helped them on their way up? Mary Kay Ash of Mary Kay Cosmetics, for one. When she first started out in sales her goal was to be the woman sales leader for the year, because she wanted to win the alligator handbag that was awarded as the prize! She also used written goals later in life when she started up her retirement business, a little sales company that grew into the Mary Kay Cosmetics corporation. Andrew Carnegie, one of the richest (and most philanthropic) men in history, is another. His written goal was to spend the first half of his life making money, and the second half of his life giving that money away!

Are those examples too big to imagine? Here is how Californian Cynthia Stewart Copier made written goals work for her. During the early '80s, the RV business Cynthia and her husband owned took a nosedive due to the price of gasoline. The bank repossessed their inventory, leaving them with a large empty sales lot. Not willing to accept defeat (or worse yet, bankruptcy!), Cynthia made herself a big sign and hung it in her barren office: *I will fill this lot with inventory in thirty days.* And then she sat down and picked up the phone and started calling folks who were advertising their used RVs in the newspaper. She invited them to bring their RVs to the lot and sell them there on consignment. And in 30 days, Cynthia accomplished her goal. She could look out the window onto a car lot filled with gleaming RVs to sell, RVs that had not cost her one penny to bring in! So let's get going with those written goals, and start down our own path to wealth and achievement.

GET STARTED WITH YOUR GOALS

How do you set goals? We guarantee that it will be one of the easiest, most pleasant tasks you will ever undertake. Goal setting is free! Goal setting is fun! And goal setting is a major step on your road to real financial success.

Choose a quiet moment to begin your goal setting. With a blank sheet of paper on the table before you and pen in hand, close your eyes and begin to picture the way you want your life to be. Let go of all assumptions and beliefs about what your present circumstances are, let go and dream big about what kinds of goals you would like to achieve. Think about all kinds of goals, they don't simply have to be monetary. It's actually better if they aren't all monetary—most wealth goals take a long time to achieve, and to keep your enthusiasm up you'll need to include goals that you can go out and achieve the very next day!

Perhaps one of the first goals that comes to mind is to *become a millionairess*. Great, write it down immediately. Don't sit there blushing at the thought, torturing yourself with questions about just how you will achieve that seemingly outrageous goal, just write it down. No one needs to know, no one will laugh, snicker, or sneer at you because you wrote down a big financial goal. Don't get hung up on how you will meet that goal, just write it down and move on to the next line.

Another goal might be to *pay down all debt*. Wonderful! Write that one down, too. Once again, don't stop to visualize the big mound of bills that fills your kitchen drawer, or think about the phone call you got last week from the credit department at Macy's. Write down that big goal and move on to the next line.

How about adding some personal goals here, or some family goals? This doesn't have to be a list of strictly financial goals (or you might want to make separate lists), this is your chance to put down on paper exactly what you'd like to achieve in the next few years in any category you choose. *Spend more time with the kids,* or perhaps *take a relaxing vacation soon,* or what about a goal to *increase professional visibility?*

How big should your list be? You might want to start working towards just a few goals, 10 or 12. Or you might want to go all out and make a big list. The dynamic inspirational speaker Mark Victor Hansen (coauthor of the *Chicken Soup for the Soul* books) suggests writing down 101 goals. A big number, to be sure, but one that he feels is a powerful number. "Don't just think it—ink it!" is his suggestion. Write down absolutely everything that you want to do. Mark says that he has a list of several thousand goals that he plans to accomplish in his lifetime. Just a few short years ago one of his goals was to *write a best-selling book.* Thirty million copies of the *Chicken Soup* books later, it sure looks like he can mark that one down as accomplished!

> *Jennifer: I attended a Mark Victor Hansen seminar some years ago. He urged us all to write down 101 goals that very night. "Don't just think it—ink it!" he advises. 101? What an enormous number it seemed to be. But I did. And of the original 101 goals that I wrote down on a notebook in my hotel room that very night—a mix of personal, financial, and professional goals—I have achieved fully 30 percent of them in the past two years. And then replaced those with new goals! I carry my list around with me all the time and review it every Monday. Years ago I scoffed at the idea of writing down goals; such a goofy idea, I thought. But hey, once I finally tried it, it has sure worked for me!*

An important part of any list of goals is the section that lists the goals that you have accomplished. Every time you look at that section you will be filled with pride and a warm sense of achievement. It will inspire you to go on and work that much harder towards achieving the goals left on your list. "But wait," you say. "How can I have a section of accomplished goals if I am just now starting to write them down?" We say, cheat. Well, don't actually cheat, but just prime the pump a bit.

Once you have written up your list of goals, no matter how big or small, get out another blank piece of paper. Across the top of this one write the word—*Accomplished!* Now, start to write down all of the major things that you have already accomplished in your life (regardless of whether you ever thought of them as goals). High school graduation? Sure, that was something that was a goal of yours as a teenager and you accomplished it. So write it down. List all other educational achievements including degrees, certificates, and professional seminars. List all career achievements—any pat on the back from the boss, any promotion or raise. Then list all personal achievements—the trails you've hiked, the good kids you raised, the nice house you keep, your prizewinning recipe for blackberry cobbler—whatever you want to pat yourself on the back for.

Once you have a nice page of accomplishments that you have already achieved in your life, clip your new goals to that page. Although some folks recommend putting your written list of goals away and letting the *power of the universe* work its magic for you, we say *keep them close at hand.* Keep your list of goals (along with that brand new list of what you have *already* achieved!) someplace where you can pull it out and look at it whenever you need to refocus and check your progress. Don't lock your goals away in a safety deposit box at the bank, put them in your underwear drawer or tuck them in a part of your briefcase.

Not only should you keep your list of goals nearby and always accessible, we think you should make your list of goals *look* grand. Once you have developed a list of goals that you feel good about, copy them onto a nice piece of stationery. Keep them in an expensive envelope, a flashy folder, or even a grand-looking gift box. Anything to make your goals look important and special whenever you view them.

Jennifer: I keep my goals with me all the time in a bright red folder that I carry in the side pocket of my book bag. The first part is called, "Goals I Set and Then Achieved!," and it is going on two pages long! Then my actual list of goals follows. Not only do I keep my list of goals in that folder, I sometimes tuck in related materials—the brochure for a spa I'd like to treat myself to, a picture of a house that I'd like to build, an article about an exclusive professional retreat that I'd like to be invited to participate in. Every Monday I open my folder and read through my goals. I make notes on the pages all the time—notes about what I can do right away that will move me closer to achieving a particular goal. My goals range from the quite mundane (redecorate master bedroom) to the very specific (fill an entire bookshelf with books I have written). From big financial goals (Peter and I will have $2 million in assets by the year 2002) to big parenting goals (raise wise sons). In my goals folder I also keep a list of 200 people that I'd like to meet. And once a week, just like clock work, I sit down and remind myself of all of these things.

HARNESS YOUR OWN HARD WORK AND BRAINPOWER

So how will all of this list making get you any closer towards being wealthy? Why are we yammering on about goals in a book about becoming a millionaire? Because in order to arrive somewhere (like financial bounty and comfort), you must know where you want to go. Because in order to truly succeed, you must be clear about what it is that you want out of life. Because achieving your goals, financial or otherwise, takes *effort,* and the best way to concentrate on putting *effort* into something is to keep your mind focused on what it is that you want to do.

And yes, all of this list making will get you closer towards your financial dreams. And it will be through your own hard work and brainpower, not the endless power of the universe. A powerful force is certainly at work, but it is your own previously untapped power that you are harnessing. Your own energy and creativity are going to work on your behalf, helping you come up with a plan to make those dreams come true.

Bettina: Some years ago when I was working on my first book, Chiquita's Cocoon, *I taped a goal to the top of my old 286 computer, just above the screen. Every day I would look at what I had written:* I want this message to be shared with women around the world. *Day in and day out I wrote the book and looked at that message. So did everyone else who came into the house, as I had rearranged my living room into a giant office. Some who saw my little sign smiled sadly at my goal, some laughed, and some urged me on. It was hard, but I just kept my mind on my goal, ignored the putdowns, and kept on working. It was harder to ignore the rejections that I was getting from publishers, though. After the first 50 I stopped counting! And I looked at my sign once again. No one would publish it? Well then, I thought, concentrating on my goal, I would publish it myself! And I did! That was a long and hard process, too, but I always returned to my written goal, to share this message with women around the world. It kept me going during many discouraging moments.*

Bettina's story raises a good point. Should you let other people know what your goals are? Or should you keep them to yourself as a private statement of your hopes and dreams? We all feel the need to protect ourselves from teasing and ridicule. If there are people in your life that you think might make fun of your goals, go ahead and keep them private for as long as you need to. Forever, if you'd like. But don't overlook the satisfaction you will one day feel when you can turn casually to someone in your life and say something like, "My goal was to start my own business within two years, and it only took me six months from the time I wrote that down!"

Some people not only share their goals with friends and family, they also place their goals all over the house in order to *really* stay focused! Like Bettina's sign taped to her computer, constantly reminding her of her pledge to herself, or Cynthia's sign posted in her empty RV sales office, if your goals are constantly within eyesight your energy and creativity will be working full time on achieving those goals.

Here's an idea. Post some of your wildest goals on your bathroom mirror. Every morning you will remind yourself of what you would like to accomplish and think, "What can I do *today* that will bring me closer to the result I want? Who can I call to help me with that goal? What action steps can I take? Where can I get the knowledge I will need to make this happen?" Imagine what you could accomplish if you put your mind to work towards achieving your goals *every single day*. You would be unstoppable!

What you can conceive and believe—you *can* achieve!

Gold, jewels, goals. Three beautiful words that you deserve to have in abundance in your life.

EXERCISE

Just getting started with writing your goals down? Here is an easy way to begin, one which will boost your confidence right away and rev you up to start working on all of the big things you want out of life.

Choose a modest goal, just a very small one to start with. You have big financial goals, of course (you deserve to!), but start with just a small one for this week. Decide that you will save $20 this week. Now, write a list of ways that you could do that—by bringing your lunch to work a few times, by carpooling or taking the subway a few days instead of driving (think of the gas savings!), or by staying away from all retail stores. Write your goal down on a piece of paper, fold it, and put it into your pocket.

Every morning, look at that piece of paper and think about your goal. At lunch time, look at that piece of paper and think about your goal. When you get undressed at night, look at that piece of paper and think about your goal.

Each time you look at that paper, your mind will be filled with ideas for new ways to save an extra $20 a week! And at the end of the week, don't be surprised if you've actually saved $40 instead! Forty dollars that you can put aside for your investment fund, $40 that you can hang onto and grow for your *I'm-starting-a-business* account.

LESSON 8

Define Yourself by the Present and the Future, Not the Past

Are you finding yourself inspired by the lessons we've shared with you so far? Inspired, but perhaps a wee bit overwhelmed? Overwhelmed, intimidated, and feeling that the examples and advice we have shared from wealthy and successful women seem not to have much to do with your life because your life is, well, not so perfect right now?

Debt? Divorce? Career problems? Relationship trouble? Feeling like you should have made different choices in your life? Or worse yet, feeling like you have no choice in your life? Put all of those feelings aside. Starting now, you will learn to define yourself by the present and the future, not by the past. Starting now you will define yourself by where you want to be financially, not by what your bank balance is at the moment.

You need to push your past away from you. Do not let your disappointment (or worse yet, your shame) about past failures hold you back from a prosperous future. Thank your past life for all of the lessons it taught you. Your past made you the woman you are at this exact moment—the woman who is holding a book called *The Millionairess Across the Street* and planning to make big changes. Everything that happened in the past made you ready for your future.

Do you sometimes feel that you are the only one with a past you would rather not mention? That everyone around you has just skated through life and never had to deal with some of the outrageous things that have happened in *your* life, and that is why they are successful and you are still at the starting gate?

Is that really how it is? Or has almost everyone at some time in their lives had to deal with disappointment and failure? Let's check in with a few extremely successful women. Did they always have it so good?

- *Mary Kay Ash.* We've used Mary Kay over and over as an example of many things. She is also a good example of a woman who suffered career failures and was passed over for advancement despite her record of achievement. But she never let the things in her past hold her back, she kept on working towards a different future.

- *Suze Orman.* The daughter of a small-time restaurant operator, Suze, at age 13, watched her father risk his life in a fire to save the cash box from his business. Suze herself spent many years as a waitress in Berkeley, California, before taking steps to change her life and become a stockbroker. And now? She is a major star on PBS and the author of two best-selling books on finance, including *The Nine Steps to Financial Freedom.*

- *Oprah Winfrey.* Does Oprah ever let herself be stopped by her past? A past which includes a poor and painful childhood, a teenage pregnancy, and an on-again-off-again weight problem? If ever a woman had a reason to stay in bed in the morning and feel sorry for herself, Oprah has it. But she has long since moved on and left these images behind, carving out a dramatically different life than the one her childhood in Kosciusko, Mississippi, seemed destined for.

- *Ivana Trump.* Publicly humiliated by her husband's tabloid love affair, Ivana fought back. First by challenging the pre-nup agreement that she had signed years before, and then by becoming a big business success! Instead of taking her divorce settlement and quietly leaving the stage, Ivana founded her own clothing and jewelry company, House of Ivana. Now with one of the most popular lines of clothing on television's QVC network, Ivana did not let her past in anyway define her present or her future.

Yes, these are all famous and accomplished women. But look closely at the successful people you admire in your community, chances are that they, too, have had to overcome obstacles in the past. No one rockets directly to the top. No one is immune from setbacks and failures. But successful people choose to continue focusing on their future instead of their past.

Still dwelling on your past mistakes? Worried that your present isn't so hot, either? Look at it this way: You are a woman who is now aware of the need for big change in her life. And *presently,* you are reading a book to help you achieve those changes! Sometimes our past failures will lead us directly to our future success!

> *Jennifer: I failed big time at my first career out of college. Politics. I just wasn't any good at it. But I'm glad that I failed so quickly, I moved into a different field after only two miserable years of trying hard to succeed. And it was that failure and un-happiness that lead me right into writing and publishing!*

Having difficulty picturing a life any different from the one you are living at this exact moment? Visualization works wonders to help you relax and imagine a different kind of life. By closing your eyes and using your own very active imagination to create a vivid picture of how you'd like your life to be, you can help convince yourself that it is something you can achieve. Serious students of visualization techniques suggest that the best results come from repetition. Set aside the same time of day (late at night, or first thing in the morning are both great times) to do your visualizing. Choose a recording of your favorite soothing music (nothing with words or lyrics, please, just plain music), dim the lights in the room, lie back on a comfortable bed or couch, and let your mind create the picture of your prosperous future.

HIT THE SHOWERS

Is visualization just a little too touchy-feely for you? We have a great little trick to help you overcome that. Take a shower. A shower? How can taking a shower can help your imagination conjure up a different sort of life? Like this:

- As you stand under the warm rushing water, close your eyes. Picture in your mind a different shower, perhaps the shower you used in a house or apartment you lived in years ago. As you stand there remembering, it is easy to clearly imagine what your life was like then. Remember what the rest of the bathroom looked like, how the towels felt on your skin. Your past life is very real to you as you stand there with your eyes closed, remembering old sights and sensations.

- Then, with your eyes still closed and the warm water enveloping you, picture your present shower. Yes, in your mind you can feel the towels and the shaggy rug that greets your feet when you climb out. Your present life is very real to you as you stand there with your eyes closed, thinking about how things look and feel now.

- Now, with your eyes closed and the warm, soothing water running over you, imagine a new life. A different life in the not too distant future. A life where you step out onto cool marble tiles and reach for a soft, plush towel. A life where, when your shower is finished, you will dress and head off to a place where your success is well known. With your eyes still closed, imagine what your future house will look like. Imagine your future circumstances—everything from your bank account to your career and your brand new mahogany lawn chairs. Go ahead and draw a detailed picture in your mind. Imagine that you are taking your shower in the future, and that when you open your eyes you will see that new life. Does it come in a little more clearly now? Can you picture your future without feeling threatened by your past or limited by your present?

Now that you're feeling the warm afterglow of your imagination shower, why not keep that warm feeling going all day? Help keep that positive, future-oriented feeling throughout the day by ignoring all of the negative messages that seem to clutter the world. Turn your car radio to a soothing classical station and daydream along to the sounds of violins. Don't listen to the news of a dreadful car wreck or the ravings of a talk show host. Ignore today's newspaper with its photos of famine and despair. We don't live in a perfect world, but there is no reason for you to steep yourself in all of this negative thought and grim reality. Let your mind soar, let your mind dwell on what wonderful things lie ahead for you.

AND ANOTHER THING

Another thing that has held many women back in the past—held them back from moving on and claiming their prosperous futures—is guilt. Large doses of guilt. We women do have a tendency to accept blame and responsibility for almost everything that goes wrong around us. And in order to move towards our future successes we need to abandon that tendency. Azriella Jaffe, small business expert and author of the forthcoming book *Take Yourself Off the Hook,* likes to remind women that "there are moments when the best thing you could do is to love your guilt instead of trying to change it." That is, if your guilt is stemming from unreasonable expectations of yourself.

So why sit around feeling burdened by guilty feelings from your past? Move on and leave it all behind. In our exercises for this lesson you will learn a great technique for shedding your past. The same goes for unnecessary guilt, it simply holds you back from attaining the future you deserve!

You have complete control over your future. Take charge now, take active steps to make sure that your future is filled with prosperity, good fortune, and success.

EXERCISES

1. Write down your biggest failures, no matter how much the memory makes you cringe. Once you have emptied your mind and your conscience of these negative experiences, close the page with the following thought: *I will no longer let these events define my present or my future.* Then tear the page (or pages) into very small pieces. Get rid of your past for good by flushing the pieces down the toilet or tossing them into the wind!

2. Write a complete description of your life as you'd like it to be five years from now. Be very detailed, include information about your friends and family, the wallpaper in the dining room, the exact type of car you'll be driving

and where you like to go in it, and the exact amount you see in the monthly statements from your investment portfolio. Once you have drawn a clear picture of your life in the future, close the page (or pages) with this thought: *My future is before me. I can shape it however I want.*

LESSON 9

Quit Squandering Your Money—Keep More to Make More!

The pictures in the women's magazines seem so seductive—all those thin, attractive women wearing the latest fashions, decked out with expensive gold and diamond jewelry, driving gleaming brand new cars. So you say to yourself, "Hey, I worked hard for my money. I deserve a little treat now, I think I'll buy that new black dress I saw advertised in *Vogue* last week. I'm a successful woman and I should dress like one so that people recognize and acknowledge my success." And when you buy that dress, spending the $400 or $500 it costs at Nordstrom, you do feel like a rich woman, don't you? And all those other women shopping at Nordstrom's with you, they must be rich too.

Guess again. Most wealthy women aren't out shopping for the latest little designer bauble they've seen advertised, they are sitting at home watching *Louis Rukeyser's Wall Street Week* on PBS while drinking a glass of inexpensive white wine. And if they do need something new (to replace something that has been worn faithfully for the past ten years or so) they are just as apt to flip open a preppy mail order catalog, choose a moderately priced outfit, and phone in the order rather than jump in the car and head over to the mall. Or better yet, if they feel the need to wear a status label, they know when the annual sales are at their favorite stores.

Need something posh-looking now and can't wait until a sale? Take a tip from California real estate entrepreneur Nikki Rueppel, head out for the nearest upscale consignment shop. "Extraordinary, the sorts of dresses you can find hanging in a designer resale shop at perfectly reasonable prices. I think it is a great way for young women to buy designer clothes without spending too much money." Unbelievable as it sounds, there really are used Chanels, Donna Karans, and St. John's Knits hanging from the racks of consignment shops all around the country waiting for you to come in and buy them for a fraction of what you would spend in a retail boutique or department store.

TAKE PRIDE IN SAVING INSTEAD OF SPENDING

Many of the women wandering through the aisles at Nordstrom's have crushing credit card bills that will be consuming their hard-earned money for years to come, preventing them from ever really getting ahead and building up any wealth. As Jennifer's mother told her many years ago, "There are two types of people, my dear. Those who have money, and those who spend money." And the wonderful thing is that, if you *have* money and have the inner confidence to know how well you are doing, then you don't feel at all inclined to buy flashy and expensive things in order to flaunt your status. No, you will take quiet satisfaction in knowing that your car might be a few years old and you've worn the same coat for several winters, but your mutual funds and your stock portfolio have been humming along nicely putting all the money you opted *not* to spend on frivolous things to work and increasing. Watch out for the much-used fashion marketing term *investment dressing*. Buying an expensive piece of clothing, regardless of how well-made or timeless the design, is *not* an investment. Create your own type of investment dressing by deciding *not* to buy an expensive piece of clothing and putting the money into the market where you can get a real return!

Some women who come from poor backgrounds feel a need to live lavishly, as if to prove to themselves and those around them that they are no longer poor. Others belong to a different school, to live comfortably but not ostentatiously. To once again quote Jennifer's mother, Mary Alice, go for "reverse snobbery." Having money, but opting not to spend it lavishly, is a type of reverse snobbery, a way of feeling quietly superior to all of those flashy folk who only can feel good about themselves by surrounding themselves with showy symbols of surface success. Rita Gibson, an art historian turned insurance and securities saleswoman, tells us that "whenever I see a young woman driving a fancy car I think to myself, 'now there is someone without a dime in the bank.' And I know that to be true in most cases. I see it over and over again with my clients. The ones who drive up in the flashiest cars are the ones who have the smallest assets. And that fancy car? It's leased!"

Another little story about cars: As a young girl, Jennifer conjured up great romantic visions of what one of her father's friends must be like. One old friend was a French count who had married into a large California ranching family, she imagined him arriving for a lunch in San Francisco in a large white Rolls Royce, or at the very least a chauffeured Cadillac limousine. And what did the count turn out to be driving? An old and dusty station wagon. Many smart and successful women follow that philosophy too. In an industry where top Wall Street players glide down the street in sleek limos, Abby Joseph Cohen, the chief equity strategist (and newly minted partner) for Goldman, Sachs & Company takes the bus to work every morning.

Why, in a motivational money book, are we haranguing you about squandering money? This is an inspirational book, shouldn't we be inspiring you to go after the things you want?

Let's go back to the front, the very front cover of this book, as a matter of fact. The subtitle reads *Women: Lessons to Change Your Thinking and Achieve Wealth and Success.* The key words here are *Achieve Wealth.* We are here to encourage you to accumulate wealth, which is entirely different from accumulating possessions. In fact, accumulating possessions undermines efforts to accumulate wealth. According to the dictionary, to accumulate means to "acquire an increasing quantity of" or, to "increase in quantity or amount." It is *money* that we want you to acquire an increasing quantity of, *money* that grows and accumulates on its own rather than being used to make a payment on your credit card!

WHAT IS HOLDING YOU BACK?

In writing this book we asked a great many wealthy women an important question: What do you think stands in the way of most women accumulating wealth? We got many different answers. One answer that we heard over and over again was women spend their windfalls on other people, rather than leaving the money alone and letting it accumulate. We like to show our love and affection for others—our children, our husbands, our friends—by giving gifts. The following is an embarrassing (for Jennifer, anyway!) example of this very impulse in action.

Jennifer: It was nearing Father's Day and my husband Peter had been dropping hints about an expensive piece of woodshop equipment that he'd like to own—an $800 bandsaw. I'd just bought 100 shares of a rapidly rising Net stock a *few days before, and came up with what I thought was a great idea. I would wait and watch the stock, and if it went up eight points (thereby rising in value by $800) I would sell the stock and buy Peter the bandsaw! That way, not only would he be pleased by the gift he'd wanted, but also by the thought that his wife was a stock market wizard. I'd feel great!*

Feel great? Maybe, but not a very clever long-term way to accumulate wealth. As it turned out, her pending mistake dawned on her in time. Peter bought his own bandsaw, and Jennifer hung on to the stock. Instead of an $800 windfall spent on someone else, the stock doubled in value in a matter of weeks and added $6,000 to her account. Ultimately more satisfying than the short-lived chance to *feel great* about giving someone else a gift. And for Father's Day? Peter got a book.

Other than our own impulse to spend on other people, what else stands in the way of many women as they try to accumulate wealth? "Frivolous spending," was another of the answers we heard from wealthy women.

We need to be aware that, 24 hours a day, we are the targets of incredible advertising and marketing campaigns designed to separate us from our hard-earned money. Every magazine, every newspaper, every billboard, and almost every television program comes jam-packed with slick advertising meant to appeal to us, to create a desire to purchase something that we never knew we needed! Advertising is what fuels the media. Of course, you as a sophisticated woman know that is what drives the magazine, newspaper, and television industries. But you also need to be aware of the messages, you need to be aware how much money and effort is being spent to encourage you as a woman to throw away the money that you worked so hard to get. All of those gorgeous ads for makeup, nail polish, earrings, hair spray, items both small and large—just think how much of your money is being tossed away on frivolous things that are being marketed to you, the American woman? The secret message of all of the advertising is to make you feel that, without this particular product or item, you are somehow inadequate, not successful, and certainly not hip. In order to be able to resist these messages and rise above them you need to work develop a thick skin, to know that even without that product you are a perfectly valuable human being.

We need to be on guard online, as well. A recent *Wall Street Journal* headline read, "Soap and Diaper Makers Pitch to Masses of Web Women." The article opened up by observing that, "As a critical mass of women logs onto the World Wide Web, consumer-marketing giants are right behind them, stepping up their online pitches for everything from soap to spaghetti sauce." Right behind us? Look over your shoulders, ladies, and hang onto your purses!

Economics professor Juliet Schor learned a shocking fact when she and a student designed a consumer buying test. Although quality tests conducted by *Consumer Reports* showed that consumers could not find large differences in quality between expensive lipsticks sold at cosmetics counters and inexpensive lipsticks available in the grocery store, Schor found that the higher the price, the *more* women tend to purchase them. Why? To literally buy status in public. So that at the end of a lunch with friends, women can reach into their purse and pull out an expensive lipstick to apply in public. A lipstick brand that their friends can recognize from across the table.

In her book *The Overspent American: Upscaling, Downshifting, and the New Consumer* (Basic Books, 1998), Schor vividly documents how our nationwide spending jag keeps so many Americans (and not just women, mind you) working hard to earn more money simply to pay the bills for the frivolous purchases they have been seduced into making.

"But wait!" you say. "Didn't I learn in Lesson 1 to *think big?!* Didn't you want me to dream and brainstorm about all of the extraordinary things that I could have in life rather than settling for whatever paltry crumbs I might have now? When do I get the diamonds, the shiny cars, and the cashmere bathrobe that I put on my *think big* list?" As real estate mogul Nikki Rueppel tells us, "To be a success you have to be willing to give up a lot of frivolous things along the way. Then when you get to be a big financial success you don't have to give up much at all!" Nikki, by the way, doesn't need to buy her Chanel suits at the consignment store.

Now, do not confuse the message of this lesson with the popular messages about *simplifying your life* or *downscaling your desires*. We just want you to understand that you need to wait for some of the good stuff in life, and that if you try to buy it too soon you will actually delay (or even derail!) your achievement of millionaire status. It takes self-discipline to inure yourself to the seductive advertising messages and ignore their *spend, spend, spend* messages. But by developing the self-discipline to resist the impulse to squander your hard-earned dollars on frivolous purchases you also will be developing self-discipline that will serve you well on your quest to become a millionairess.

Another insidious form of advertising is now targeted to women—the *get rich quick* and *work from home* schemes. With so many women seeking ways to increase their incomes or start their own businesses, sharp marketers have filled the back pages of women's magazines with ads for businesses with high entry costs and little chance for success. Read books for money? Don't count on it. Make crafts from home? We wouldn't. Cast a skeptical eye on any of these kinds of approaches. Women are once again being preyed upon as easy marks, being treated as silly things who will spend their money on a hope and a prayer. Don't fall for it. Spend your money and your time developing your own ideas.

DON'T LET TELEVISION
SEDUCE YOU TO SPEND

While we are on the topic of squandering, let's briefly touch on another precious thing that can all too easily be squandered—time. Just as no one ever got rich going shopping, no one ever got rich just sitting in front of the television set hour after hour. Even Oprah Winfrey, queen of the small screen, avoids watching television. "It promotes false values," she says. So take a hint from an enormously wealthy and successful woman, turn off that TV and get up off of that couch.

To once again cite the work of Juliet Schor in *The Overspent American,* she documents a link between the amount of television watching and overspending. The more TV you watch, the less you save. Each hour of television a week reduces your annual savings by $208. And it is not just the commercials that viewers are exposed to that encourages overspending—it is the shows themselves. She believes that many popular television shows promote upper-class spending patterns that few Americans can match. Remember *Dallas? Dynasty?* Hmmm, she's got quite a point there!

Not only will turning off the television spare you all of those seductive advertising messages, it also will free up lots of time for brainstorming business and investment ideas!

EXERCISES

1. Here is a way to get a handle on just how all of those little frivolous purchases can add up and eat away at the money you could be using for wealth-creation. Take a

copy of your favorite magazine and start to write in it the prices of everything you see advertised. Everything from a tube of lipstick or a wand of mascara to the really big items like jewelry and fashion. The sum total of everything advertised in an issue of, say, *Vanity Fair,* could easily approach a million dollars. Or watch television for an evening with a pad of paper and a pencil, writing down the dollar value of everything that is advertised that night—takeout meals from McDonald's, brand new cars from Buick, a different kind of household cleaner. It does add up, doesn't it? And was any of what you saw advertised really anything that you *needed?* Probably not.

The more you become aware of advertisers' attempts to create a longing and desire for their products, the better able you will be to pass up those small (or big!) things that you really don't need. The money you don't spend on those things will work hard for you once you put it in the stock market, invest it in starting your own business, or buy a rental property. You worked hard for your money, now make your money work hard for you. As *The Wall Street Journal* noted recently in an article on retirement nest eggs, "Nobody ever got rich by going shopping." Remember that the next time you are considering a frivolous purchase.

2. Here is another eye-opener. Think back over the past six months. Did you make a large purchase that you now regret? A fancy coat that never got worn? An expensive piece of stereo equipment that you never use? Or a large and extravagant gift that you bought for a loved one? Just exactly how much did you spend on it?

   Now let's do a simple math exercise. If instead of buying that $750 dollar coat, you'd invested the money, what would that sum grow to over the years?

- $750.00 invested at 10 percent would grow to $825.00 in one year.
- $825.00 invested at 10 percent would grow to $907.50 in the second year.
- $907.50 invested at 10 percent would grow to $998.30 in the third year.
- $998.30 invested at 10 percent would grow to $1,098.10 in the fourth year.
- $1,098.10 invested at 10 percent would grow to $1,208.00 in the fifth year.
- $1,208.00 invested at 10 percent would grow to $2,063.00 in the tenth year.
- $2,063.00 invested at 10 percent would grow to $3,320.70 in fifteenth year.
- $3,320.70 invested at 10 percent would grow to $5,347.65 in twentieth year.

So, which was the better idea? Buying that new coat or hanging on to that money and investing it? Remember: *Accumulate* is the name of the wealth game.

Get with the Wealth Boom—Join the New Economy of Ideas!

Everyone is doing it—developing ideas, plotting strategies, raising capital, and *making millions.* You can hardly pick up a newspaper or magazine or listen to the news without learning about someone becoming an *instant-aire* through invention, technology, communications, investments, information, or some radically new idea. The phrase, "That's a great money-making idea!" defines this lesson. Why shouldn't you be out there too looking for your way to jump on board? Let's meet some of the gutsy women who took their ideas all the way to the top. And don't be intimidated by these high-powered examples—be inspired! Be inspired and courageous enough to try it for yourself. Here we go.

Beginning with a simple invention and parlaying it into millions, few have done it as well as Tomima Edmark. A marketing representative for IBM, Tomima was sitting in a movie theater when she spotted a woman with an unusual twisted ponytail hairstyle. Realizing that she had spotted a marketable idea,

Tomima experimented at home until she came up with a winning device. Her Topsy Tail has gone on to sell $100 million worth of product. What exactly did Tomima do? She took a big chance and ran her own two minute infomercial, selling 3.6 million units this way! "What you have to do," she explains, "is from the moment you get your idea, you have to start your research on how to develop, protect (patent), produce (manufacture), fund, advertise, distribute, and fill orders. I wasn't an expert on any of these things but I sure became one fast." Today, Tomima advises entrepreneurs nationwide through "Bright Ideas," a monthly column for *Entrepreneur* magazine. Need advice on how to develop your bright ideas? Pick up your pen and write to her.

In the fast-paced world of technology, women are no exception. The very first commercial site on the World Wide Web was Global Network Navigator. Founder and CEO Lisa Gansky sold her site to America Online in 1995. Her advice in these super-competitive times is to "build a network of talented people to think and grow with."

Pamela Lopker (who made the front cover of *Forbes* in 1996) is this country's richest self-made woman; the "*Forbes* Four Hundred" lists her fortune at an extremely inspiring $425 million. How did she make it? She started QAD, a computer programming business that developed inventory, accounting, and order tracking software. From a seemingly innocuous idea—tracking orders for shoemakers—Lopker found a need and filled it in a big, big way.

Nike has paid off for Sheryl Swoopes too. She is the first woman to have an athletic shoe named after her. The Olympic gold medalist-turned WNBA basketball star collected $2 million from Nike for her endorsement of the Air Swoopes. Who's next?

The WNBA wasn't a slam dunk for just Sheryl Swoopes though, the three founders of Girl World Sports, Inc. in Houston have made a couple of three point shots themselves. Launched in 1996 by Bridget Degan, Ellen Krantz, and Sasha Milby, the $3 million apparel company has an exclusive contract for the official WNBA T-shirt line. The partners also rack up big sales with baseball caps emblazoned "Go Girl" and colorful T-shirts with slogans like "Games Real Girls Play" and "Girls Rule the Court."

We may as well shoe-in another success story here. California triathelete Sally Edwards turned her '70s jogging passion into an 80s athletic shoe business that raced to success and fortune with the aptly named Fleet Feet. She built it into a franchise company before selling out for big money. She really *did* do what she loved and the money *did* follow!

We could go on all day about the incredible success women are having, but let's just examine two more. In 1992 mail order entrepreneur Barbara Todd figured out a cheaper, better way to get her Oregon-based Good Catalog Company off the ground—she charged manufacturers up front for space in her catalog! And how's she doing now? How does $30 million a year sound?

And when Grace Reyes had trouble getting her young son to take his medicine, she found a way to lick the problem. She came up with a better way to give it to him—in a lollipop. Her company, Naturally Made Products, is close to earning $5 million a year. A sweet victory.

COMBINE INSPIRATION WITH PERSPIRATION

Ideas, ideas. Ideas come in many forms and are everywhere around you. You can go looking for them, you can stumble across them, they can be offered to you, or you might already have them in you just ready to hatch. The reality is that in order to be successful and get rich you have to put your idea out into the commercial world. Your inspiration will be followed by lots of perspiration and you will need both time and money. Any idea worth pursuing can be fully realized and accomplished step by step when you remain mentally focused and ready to accept the constant challenge.

Suppose you're not ready to risk your signature on a multi-million dollar lending note. What then? Where will you find the money? Well, take a cue from Janice Davidson who, after being stood up by a software publisher at lunch in 1982, raided $6,000 from her children's college fund to get her educational software business going. Her husband Robert, a construction executive, persuaded her not to accept the snub from the industry but to go ahead and publish the program herself. Jan's program Speed Reader was a quick hit—5,400 copies the first year. By 1986 sales were $4 million a year, and in July of 1996 the Davidsons sold their company for $1 billion. "And we were worried about wiping out the kids' savings," Jan says.

Okay, so you don't want to raid your children's college fund. How about some plain old-fashioned hustle and creative ingenuity? After five years of secretarial work and no job in her field, college graduate Karen Bell became frustrated by her precarious financial situation. "Things were really tight for me," Bell said. "So I started racking my brain trying to think of something I could do to bring in extra cash. Sitting on the floor staring at my feet, the idea of socks hit me. Socks were the only thing I could afford because they had a low price tag."

With just $30 to "waste," as she puts it, Bell walked into her local department store and purchased a dozen plain white women's socks. "I bought them on sale, took them out of their packaging, and sewed buttons on them and put rhinestones on their cuffs." Next, this courageous entrepreneur donned her best outfit and hit the pavement on Rodeo Drive in Beverly Hills, the famous shopping street of the superwealthy. Karen had planned to spend some time presenting the socks to merchandise buyers in the boutiques in the area, but was able to call it a day after her first sales pitch. "The owner flipped over them," reports Bell, "I couldn't believe it when he bought all my socks for $60—double what I had paid for them." With every successful sale she got bolder and bolder, but, she cautions, "I kept my day job and filled orders at night. I had trouble obtaining a credit line from the bank so I borrowed as much as $50,000 from a friend and repaid it with interest. Now my bank credit line is at the $300,000 level." Talk about socking it away! Today her hosiery company, K. Bell, pulls in $5 million a year.

What's that, you say? You are one of those people who never has a good idea? Phooey. Ever come up with an idea for a movie? Where would Hollywood be without writers? There is no secret formula to becoming a millionaire through media rich ideas. Television shows and movies come from ideas, stories, and experiences that have been translated onto film. Can you find a way to get involved? If your idea antennae is receiving this, you owe it to yourself to pick up a copy of *Variety,* the movie and television trade newspaper. The weekly money talk that marches across the pages is almost obscene, but it does wonders for your millionaire motivation.

GOING PUBLIC

Another way (albeit a real long shot) to get with the wealth boom and become rich is in the stock market, which despite dizzying ups and downs has created fortunes for many small investors with the nerve to stay in the game. Own a company? The idea is to let others make you rich by getting them to invest in your company. Here's how. Let's say you own 80 percent of your company, it's doing well but you need to raise more cash. You decide to *go public*—to sell stock in your company to the general public. If, after much regulatory hoopla, financial scrutiny, and mounds of paperwork, your initial public offering (IPO) is successful, you as a large shareholder can really cash in. Although managing an IPO is a complex chorus of company founders, backers, investors, hard work, patience, vision, and readiness, it is definitely the newest American gold rush.

Don't yet own a company that you can take public? Well then, start researching good publicly traded companies you can buy stock in. The summer of 1998 saw enormous gains in the value of *Net stocks,* companies who did business on the Internet. Companies like bookseller Amazon.com and search engine Yahoo! were suddenly the stars of the stock market as their stock soared, doubling and sometimes tripling in a matter of a few short weeks. After peaking on July 17th, the market went into a steep decline for the rest of the summer and most of the fall before rallying again. Is this scenario likely to happen again? Who knows, but keep your eyes open for opportunities to invest in the good ideas of other business pioneers. Bettina did.

> *Bettina: In December 1998, when CBS took its radio division—Infinity—public, my daughter and I glued ourselves to stock market news and literally heard our investment grow by the hour. It was incredibly exciting to be a part of the third largest IPO in history!*

In the world of financial services, 35-year-old Abigal Johnson is poised to pick up a chunky gold nugget. Her father Ned owns Fidelity, the multibillion dollar mutual fund company, and Abigal has been steadily working her way up through the ranks in order to someday run the whole show. Yes, Abigal is in a class by herself, but her neighborhood—Wall Street—is open to everyone.

Such a deal! America is booming for women everywhere. No matter where your interests, talents, and skills lie, your opportunity for becoming a millionairess is *now*. In your favor is the fact that everything has shifted from the business of manufacturing things to the business of thinking things up, drastically cutting the time it takes to build a fortune. And what is the greatest reward of business ownership for women? Gaining absolute control over their own fate.

Georgia Jones took a close look at her daily life as a stay-at-home mom and founded a company as a result. She noticed that she spent a fair amount of time telling her friends how to use their computers. Hmmm, was that something she should charge for? Yes! Georgia Jones formed a company called Computer Moms, which recruits stay-at-home moms to become computer consultants. Check out their Web site at www.computermoms. com! And keep your own eyes open for business opportunities every day.

EXERCISES

How can you find that special idea that will rocket you to the top of the new economy of ideas? Here are five ways to spark your thinking and help you discover how to build your own wealth boom.

1. Seek out opportunities 24 hours a day. Carry a small notebook or miniature tape recorder with you at all times and make a note whenever something catches your eye, anything from noticing that there seems to be a need for a particular type of product or a better way of doing things to a brainstorm that hits you because of something you overheard in the line at the grocery store.

2. Ask yourself and your friends, "What would make my life easier?" A few years ago an enterprising Texas woman spotted a need for an entertaining television show that would keep toddlers occupied—hello, Barney the purple dinosaur!

3. Understand and use the profit principle. Before embarking on developing a new idea, product, or service, always stop and ask yourself, "Just how big can this get?" Not all businesses, products, or services really have the potential to grow to millionaire size. Be ruthless in first

assessing whether your idea will get you to your goal. Also be realistic and clear-eyed when assessing the chances for large success. Go outside your comfort circle of friends and relatives when asking for feedback and opinion. You need honest criticism, not useless flattery.

4. Open your mind to new ideas. Read the new business magazines that are geared to high-tech business and the fast-paced, modern business environment. Check your local newsstand for magazines like *Fast Company* and *Business 2.0*. Both are chock-full of articles about new businesses, young entrepreneurs, and what is really happening out there in the business world. Read, absorb, and ponder.

5. Act now! Put this book down and spend the next hour with your notebook (see Exercise 1)! Brainstorm big ideas that could change the world (like a new type of technology), small ideas that could change your neighborhood (like a faster way to drop off drycleaning), or medium-sized ideas that could change the way folks work (like a modular home office system). Don't worry about failure or embarrassment, just write things down without editing your thoughts. Becoming a millionairess is a step-by-step process, and the first step is the hardest. Take your pen in hand and take that first step now!

Learn All You Can about Women's Wealth and History

But history, real solemn history, I cannot be interested in . . . I read it a little as a duty, but it tells me nothing that does not either vex or weary me. The quarrels of popes and kings, with wars or pestilence's, in every page: the men all so good for nothing, and hardly any women at all—it is very tiresome.
—Catherine Morland in Jane Austen's *Northanger Abbey* (1817)

Motivation to become a millionairess can come from a variety of sources, but there's nothing like a little history to show us it's been done before and we can do it again. The subject of women's history together with money is important because *her wealth story* has yet to be told comprehensively. And make no mistake, women and money are a winning combination. This lesson, like this book, will show you some women's monetary achievements. For starters, did you know that the word money actually has a female origin? In mythology, it is derived from the Roman goddess Moneta, meaning riches, plenty, abundance!

Then there was Lady Godiva in 1040. Legend tells us she rode naked on horseback with only her long hair to cover her. A local merchant peeped at her and he went blind. The real story? Godiva only agreed to ride naked as part of bargain with her husband, the Earl, to get him to repeal the taxes oppressing the citizens of Coventry, which he did.

One 15th-century woman who risked and invested in the dream of a new world was, of course, Castile's Queen Isabella who pledged her jewels as security to finance Columbus on his voyage of discovery. (Was she fiercely in love with him? Well, she had to keep things interesting.)

To date, royalty still holds. The richest woman in the world today is Queen Elizabeth II. Her jewels and art are worth $5.4 billion. Worldwide, there are 20 female billionaires (and hundreds of males):

1. Queen Elizabeth II, $5.4 billion
2. Helen R. Walton, $4.9 billion
3. Alice R. Walton, $4.9 billion
4. Liliane Bettencourt, $3.7 billion
5. Grete Schickedanz, $3.5 billion
6. Estée Lauder, $3.3 billion
7. Shigeko Shino, $3.2 billion
8. Jacqueline Vogel, $2.9 billion
9. Anne Cox Chambers, $2.5 billion
10. Barbara Cox Anthony, $2.5 billion
11. Chantel Grundig, $2.4 billion
12. Heidi Horton, $1.9 billion
13. Imelda Marcos, $1.6 billion
14. Johanna Quandt, $1.5 billion
15. Susanne Klatten, $1.5 billion
16. Mary Alice Dorrance Malone, $1.4 billion
17. Laura Azcarrago de Wachsman, $1.3 billion
18. Joan Beverly Kroc, $1.2 billion
19. Kathryn McCurry Albertson, $1.1 billion
20. Margaret H. Hill, $1 billion

Whew! An impressive amount of money!

Another woman in the money, whose popular autograph you carry in your wallet although she's not wealthy in her own right, is Mary Ellen Withrow. She is the 40th treasurer of the United States and the first person to have held the post of treasurer at all three levels of government—local, state, and national. During her tenure as Ohio's treasurer, Withrow's innovative programs, management efficiencies, and record earnings for Ohio earned her nationwide recognition. An inductee into the Ohio Women's Hall of Fame, she also received the Donald L. Scantelbury Memorial Award for financial excellence and improvement in government.

Mary Ellen Withrow is preceded by 11 female U.S. treasurers: Catalina Vasquez Villapando, Texas; Katherine D. Ortega, New Mexico; Angela Marie Buchanan, District of Columbia; Azie Taylor Morton, Texas; Ramona Acosta Banuelos, California; Dorothy Andrews Elston Kabis, Delaware; Kathryn O'Hay Granahan, Pennsylvania; Elizabeth Rudel Smith, California; Ivy Baker Priest, Utah; and Georgia Neese Clark, Kansas.

TAKE A STROLL THROUGH THE PAST

In the movement of women's ideas and progress and money, historical perspectives are fascinating. Here's a stroll through the past, courtesy of *The Women's Chronology* by James Trager (reprinted by permission of Henry Holt and Company):

- *1870.* Victoria Clafin Woodhull, 32, and her sister Tennessee Celeste Claflin, 24, establish the first women's brokerage firm on Wall Street. Daughters of an Ohio peddler and his spiritualist wife, they grew up with eight siblings in a world of medicine shows and theatrical troupes. Scandalous stories circulate about them but they gain the support of railroad magnate Cornelius Vanderbilt, and their offices open February 4, 1870, at 44 Broad Street, in New York City. They attract a crowd of some 4,000 curious visitors and within a few months they rake in over $500,000.

In 1872, Victoria announces her candidacy for U.S. presidency. She calls on all activist women to register and vote, contending that the 14th Amendment, ratified in 1868, actually enfranchised women, because it made no mention of gender in its provision asserting the rights of citizenship, and there is therefore no necessity for a 16th Amendment to grant woman suffrage. She makes a fortune on Wall Street but is unable to get onto the ballot.

- *1876.* Mary Ann Magnin, a Dutch-American seamstress opens the Yankee Notions Store that later will become San Francisco's I. Magnin. Her needles, pins, threads, and buttons have no special distinction, but Magnin attracts a wide following with the bridal trousseaux and infant layettes that she makes while raising seven children and running the shop. The Magnin family ultimately builds a nationwide chain.

- *1902.* "History of the Standard Oil Company" by journalist Ida Minerva Tarbell, 44, appears in *McClure's* in installments, revealing that John D. Rockefeller controls 90 percent of U.S. oil refining capacity and has an annual income of $45 million. Raised by a father who made a fortune building barrels for the oil trade, Tarbell uncovers facts about the secretive Rockefeller that leads to the breakup of his Standard Oil trust by the Supreme Court in 1911. But this doesn't make her any money.

- *1907.* Carrie Neiman stocks a Dallas Neiman-Marcus store with $17,000 worth of women's clothing including tailored suits, evening gowns, furs, coats, dresses, and millinery. Her inventory nearly sells out in a month and the rest is history. The $17,000? A part of the cash her husband, A.L Neiman, and his brother-in law, Herbert Marcus, received from a buyout from Coca-Cola.

- *1910.* Florence Nightingale Graham, 25, a Canadian-American beauty shop secretary, starts the Elizabeth Arden beauty salon chain in a New York beauty treatment parlor. After a falling out with her business partner, she borrows $6,000 from a cousin and opens a Fifth Avenue shop under the name Elizabeth Arden, inspired by the 1864 poem "Enoch Arden." Graham repays the loan within four months, moves farther uptown, and later opens a Washington, D.C., branch in 1915. She helps formulate the first non-greasy skin cream and packages it under the name Amoretta. Later she introduces lipsticks in colors coordinated to skin tones and clothing. By 1938 there are 29 Elizabeth Arden salons—10 of them in foreign countries—while Graham's Maine vacation home operates as a health resort under the name Maine Chance Farm. Elizabeth Arden beauty products are still best sellers in major department stores.

- *1910.* "Madame C.J. Walker," Sara Walker (nee Breedlove), 42, devises a formula for straightening tightly curled hair—the Walker Hair Method (Vegetable Shampoo, Glossine, Wonderful Hair Grower)—and sells it by mail order. Orphaned before she was 6, married at age 14, and widowed at 20, Walker works as a St. Louis washerwoman to support herself and her daughter, A'lelia, while educating herself in her spare time. She also sells her products door to door, then later lines up factories in Denver and Pittsburgh to produce them and recruits a sales force of *beauty analysts* who go from house to house dressed in white shirts and long black skirts. Five years later, her company, Mme. C.J. Walker Manufacturing Co., moves into its own Indianapolis building and prospers. Walker becomes the first black woman millionaire.

- *1912.* Above the stricken S.S. Titanic, survivor and heroine Molly Brown, 44, a millionaire in silver mining, dons woolen underwear, heavy bloomers, two wool petticoats, a $4,000 sable muff, and a $60,000 chinchilla cape, which

she gives to the shivering women and children after mar-
shalling them into the life boats. Down to her underwear,
and armed with a Colt 45, she orders them to stop crying
and start rowing. Lady Lucille Duff Gordon, another
wealthy survivor, is credited as the first dress designer to
use mannequins and the first to have models move around
in her London, Paris, and New York shops. Ida Straus, 67,
prominent millionaire of Macy's Department stores refuses
to board a lifeboat, preferring to perish with her husband.

- *1914.* Miriam Leslie, who inherited the popular (but bank-
rupt) *Leslie's Illustrator* newspaper in 1880, dies at age 78.
Having worked hard to turn the business around, she
leaves an estate of $9 million to the International Woman
Suffrage Alliance.

- *1914.* Mary Phelps (later Careese Crosby), 21, a New York
debutante, patents her design for the backless brassiere that
will replace the ubiquitous corset. She derives the backless
brassiere from two hankies and some ribbon. Friends request bras for themselves. Later, a manufacturer requests a
sample and encloses a dollar. With this encouragement she
engages a designer to make drawings, borrows $4,100,
rents two sewing machines, and hires two immigrant girls
to stitch up a few hundred backless brassieres. She takes
them to New York's better stores but meets with little success. Through a family friend she sells her patent for
$1,500 to Warner Brothers Corset Company of Bridgeport,
Connecticut. Although the value of the patent was later estimated to be $15 million she did not receive any addi-
tional payments. Though Crosby is cited as being one of
the many claimants to the title inventor of the bra, laurels
go to Parisian Herminie Cadolle. Crosby's was not the first
brassiere, per se, but as the first backless one, it was revo-
lutionary. Still, she should have been a tougher negotiator.

- *1916.* Henrietta "Hetty" Green dies at age 80 leaving an
estate of more than $100 million making her the richest

woman in America at that time. She starts her fortune with a $29 million inheritance and multiplies it with investments in stocks, bonds, mortgages, and Chicago real estate.

- *1920.* Frieda Muller Loehmann, 47, a coat buyer for A.T. Stewart & Co., and her son Charles invest $800 to open a Brooklyn shop. It has limited success until she converts it into a discount store. Using cash, she buys surplus dresses for a song from garment makers on Manhattan's cash-short 7th Avenue, and passes the savings on to her customers. She shifts entirely to discounting in 1922, and pursues bargains until two weeks before her death in 1962, at 89. By then, her Loehmann's stores have annual sales of $3 million.

- *1930.* Heiress Elanor "Cissy" Patterson Schlesinger offers to buy William Randolph Hearst's *Washington Herald*. Instead, she is hired as editor at $200 per week plus one-third of all profits. She has her name legally changed to Eleanor Medill Patterson, and reports for work August 30 in a chauffeur driven 16-cylinder Cadillac limousine. Emphasizing sex and gossip, she makes the *Herald* Washington's largest circulation morning paper within a year.

- *1933.* Brooklyn inventor Marie Wittman sells the patent rights for her Dy-Dee-Doll that takes water from a bottle and wets its diaper. It is introduced by New York's Effanee Doll Co., which sells more than 25,000 in its first year.

- *1936.* Eleanor Roosevelt contracts with the United Features newspaper syndicate to write six columns a week under the title "My Day." It is the first time a sitting first lady earns money, and her decision creates some controversy. By year's end, 60 newspapers (up from an initial 20) carry the column, including some owned by publishers who oppose FDR. Mrs. Roosevelt urges women to put family life first, but concedes that they have a right to work for personal as well as economic reasons.

- *1937.* Actress Marion Davies saves her longtime lover William Randolph Hearst from bankruptcy by giving him a

certified check for $1 million. *Washington Herald* editor
Cissy Patterson gives him an equal amount, but because
he is still in dire straits she leases the paper from him, as
well as Hearst's *Washington Times,* both for a five-year period with an option to buy. Asked about the problems of a
woman publisher, she tells an interviewer, "Men are not all
sensitive about taking a woman's money, but they don't
like to work for her. Sometimes one can overcome this by
persuasion, sometimes it takes violent methods, but the
woman must not let herself be licked." In 1939, she exercises her option and buys the *Washington Herald* and
Washington Times from William Randolph Hearst. She
merges the morning and afternoon papers to create the
Times-Herald, which has ten editions per day promoting
her isolationist views. She remains the publisher until her
death in July 1948.

- *1937.* Dorothy Shaver is promoted to president of Lord &
Taylor. While the press proclaims her $110,000 salary is the
highest on record for any woman, *Life* magazine notes that
men in comparable jobs earn four times that much. Shaver
boosts current sales of $30 million up to $50 million by
1951, and they will reach $100 million by the time of her
death in 1959.

- *1937.* Connecticut entrepreneur Margaret Rudkin (nee
Fogarty), 40, introduces Pepperidge Farm bread. She sets
up an oven in her stockbroker husband's former polo
pony stable on the family's 120-acre Pepperidge Farm, and
bakes whole wheat bread, which she sells first to neighbors and then through a New York City fancy food retailer.
Within three years, increasing demand obliges her to rent
some buildings in Norwalk, Connecticut, to expand her
baking facilities.

- *1946.* Estée Lauder, 38, makes her first sale to Saks Fifth
Avenue. The New York beautician, born Josephine Esther

Mentzer, and her husband Joseph, also 38, make and market cosmetics that grow to outsell those of Elizabeth Arden, Helen Rubinstein, and Revlon.

Next, we offer two very different stories about inventors. The contrast shows the importance of controlling your own ideas. When you do that, you control your destiny.

In 1956, Bette Claire Nesmith (nee McMurray), 32, a divorcee and typist for Texas Bank and Trust, applies for a patent and trademark on a product designed to cover up typing errors. Noticing a lettering artist using paint to conceal a mistake, she put some white tempera waterbase paint in a bottle and applied it with a watercolor brush. She called it Mistake Out. Coworkers asked for bottles of their own and Nesmith worked nights and weekends improving the correction fluid formula in her kitchen.

She offered the idea to IBM, which rejected it, so she turned her garage into a bottling factory. Soon she was selling 100 bottles per month, but she kept her job until she was fired for accidentally typing The Liquid Paper Company instead of her employer's name at the bottom of a letter.

In 1968, Liquid Paper sold more than 10,000 bottles per day and grossed more than $1 million. By 1975, she employed more than 200 people to produce 25 million bottles of Liquid Paper that she sold in 31 countries. In 1979, Gillette bought Liquid Paper for $47.5 million, plus a royalty to Bette, the one time typist, on every bottle sold until the year 2000. When she died in May 1980 at age 56, her estate was worth $50 million.

In 1965, Ruth Siems, who had a bachelor of science degree in Home Economics from Purdue University, was an employee of General Foods. In the '60s, millions of women entered the workforce, and General Foods, which stocked its inventory with ready-made foods like Bird's Eye frozen vegetables and Minute Rice, insisted on developing a bread stuffing that would cook in 15 minutes. Ruth devised the recipe for what became one of the company's top sellers, Stove Top Stuffing. Although she was technically listed as coholder of the Stove Top patent, she quickly learned that her financial rewards were minimal at General Foods: $25 upon application for a patent; $100 when the patent was obtained.

Though the company normally gave substantial bonuses to research managers for products that yielded large profits, they offered her none because she was not a manager, only a home economist. When her name was later submitted for such recognition, she was told that by inventing she was "only doing her job." When the one-billionth package of Stove Top Stuffing came off the line, the company (now held by Phillip Morris) passed out T-shirts to mark the occasion. Because no one thought to send one to the product's inventor, she ordered one for herself. Across its front was emblazoned, "With Stove Top 1984—1 Billionth Package"; on its back were the words, "Stuff It." To which the unheralded inventor replied, "Touché. My feelings exactly." Siems was even denied the laurels she would have received had she been a man. On February 9, 1997, *Parade* reported Philip Zaffere was the inventor of Stove Top stuffing.

What do we learn from these stories? You may think it's all luck but as someone once said, "The harder I work, the luckier I get." And luck is what happens to those who are well prepared.

Prepare yourself by reading, listening, and learning. Be ready for your luck by networking with successful women.

EXERCISES

1. Seek out the biographies of well-known women like Katherine Graham, and learn all you can about how they handled the business challenges they faced.

2. Remember three times when you were lucky and three times when you were unlucky. Was being prepared (or not prepared) part of your luck?

3. Whenever money is involved, be sure to spell out your rights legally. Whether you are buying a car, cosigning a lease on an apartment, or executing a contract to buy or offer goods or services, get it in writing. Think of three incidents you know where things were not spelled out.

Read and Learn All You Can about Big Business—Capitalism

Capitalism and *capitalist* are words we think we understand but may not be able to define exactly. Webster, however, clears it up for us.

Capitalism: An economic system, characterized by a free market and open competition, in which goods are produced for profit, labor is performed for wages, and the means of production and distribution are privately owned.
Capitalist: 1. An investor of capital in business. 2. One who supports capitalism. 3. A person of great wealth.
Capital: The loot.

In its pure form, capitalism is business and business is capitalism. Here is an illustration of well-developed capitalism that will blow you away. Reprinted with permission from *That's a Great Idea* by Tony Husch (Ten Speed Press, Berkeley, CA).

General Mills began in 1928 with Wheaties and Betty Crocker Flour. Sixty years later, General Mills owns the following brands (subject to recent acquisitions and divestitures): Country Corn Flakes, Breakfast Squares, Lucky Charms, Fun Pack, Kix, Nature Valley granola bars, Cheerios, Cocoa Puffs, Total, Corn Total, Yoplait yogurt, Crazy Cow, Wheaties, Andy Capp's potato snacks, Franken Berry, Buc Wheats, Kaboom, BooBerry, Frosty's, Fruit Brute, Golden Grahams, Trix, Count Chocula, Gold Medal Flour, Red Band flour, SlimJim sausages and beef jerky, Potato Buds, Gold Medal Wondra, La Pina, Complete Pancake Mix, Jesse Jones meats, O-Cel-O sponges, Bacos imitation bacon bits, Betty Crocker baking mixes and potato casseroles, Bisquick mixes, Tom's snack products, Pioneer Products cake decorations and novelties, Hamburger Helper, Tuna Helper, Mug-O-Lunch, Gorton's frozen seafood, Saluto frozen Italian foods, Pemmican beef jerky, Louise's Home-Style ravioli company, Penrose pickled meats, Good Earth Restaurants, Red Lobster Inns, Betty Crocker Pie Shops, York Steak Houses, Casa Gallardo, Fennimore's, Hannahan's, LeeWards Creative Crafts hobby supplies, Wallpapers to Go, Kittinger English furniture reproductions, Eddie Bauer sports equipment, Pennsylvania House and Dunbar Furniture, Monopoly, Clue, Happy Days, Pay, Ouiji, Sorry, Bonkers, Boogle, Nerf, Lionel trains, Craft Master paint-by-number sets, Playdoh, MPC model kits, Discovery Time preschool toys, Darci Cover Girl, Baby Alive, Easy Bake Ovens, Spirograph toys, Give-A-Show projectors, Merlin, Sector, Star Wars toys, Talbots clothing, David Crystal apparel, Monet costume jewelry, Ciani jewelry, Haymaker, Crystal sunflowers, Lord Jeff clothing, Ship'n Shore apparel, Foot-Joy gold shoes, Chemise Lacoste, and Izod fashions.

Does this open up your millionairess mind?

Capitalism is indeed exciting, adventurous, and full of drama. To know and feel this all you really have to do is read *The Wall*

Street Journal. Their articles feature global capitalism from airplanes to utilities.

BOEING REPORTS PROFIT OF $347 MILLION
REVERSING A LOSS FROM A YEAR EARLIER
Boeing Co. posted $347 million in third quarter earnings, reversing a record year-earlier loss and beating diminished Wall Street expectations largely because of a one-time tax credit . . .

PACT SIGNED FOR ACQUISITION OF
CARDIOGENESIS STOCK
Eclipse Surgical Technologies, Inc., Sunnyvale, California, said it signed a definitive agreement to acquire CardioGenesis for stock valued at about $30.4 million. Both companies make devices to treat cardiovascualr disease and angina with lasers . . .

U.S. PHONE GIANTS FIND TELMEX CAN BE
A BRUISING COMPETITOR
Mexico City. When they started up long-distance businesses in Mexico last year, U.S. phone giants AT&T and MCI thought they would teach Telefonos de Mexico SA a thing or two about competition. Instead, Telemex, as the former state-owned monopoly is called, has taught them a thing or two about doing business in the developing world . . .

Check out these *WSJ* headlines—no doubt some will hit home:

- Home-Ownership Rate Rose to Record 66.8% in Quarter
- Sears Profit Plummets by 88%, but Beats Expectations
- Merger [NationsBank and BankAmerica] Has a Rocky Start with Upset Directors and Bicostal Friction
- NFL Cancels Bond Offering Amid Investor Uncertainty
- Superior Telecom Agrees to Buy Essex for $936 million

- IBM Plans to Unveil Aptiva Model for $599 by Late Next Month
- MGM to Acquire 1,300 Polygram Films from Canada's Seagram for $235 Million
- Michael Jackson Enters Discussions on Casino Venture
- CDnow, N2K Agree to Merge and Form Dominant Web Seller

Just a few fascinating features that describe and keep the world of big business turning, trading, merging, winning, losing, profiting, rising, gaining, buying, selling, declaring, dealing, agreeing, disagreeing, risking, and marketing, and all with competitive players in a fast forward game of musical chairs.

Is big business your cup of tea? Well, it should be. What big businesses do affects our professional and personal lives. And, as writers, Bettina's and Jennifer's lives are no exception. The following two pieces in the *WSJ* certainly caught our attention:

DOWNLOADING DOSTOEVSKI: CONSUMERS TO GET A LOOK AT THE PAPERLESS BOOK
It's called NuvoMedia's Rocket ebook, priced at $499, weighs 22 ounces, and will pack some 4,000 pages of text and graphics. The books themselves will cost $18 to $25.

(Oh, oh, did we or did we not retain those electronic rights?) But then again, there's more money-making opportunity:

BOOK SAMPLES TO BE SERVED WITH DIET COKE
Coca-Cola, America's No. 1, most admired company, is teaming up with book publishers (Random House, HarperCollins, Doubleday, Penguin, Putnam) to place free excerpts of new books in 12-packs and 24-packs of Diet Coke, the nation's No. 3 soft drink. Diet Coke drinkers are mostly adults, more specifically—60% women and 40% men. The question is: will

consumers pick a 12-pack of Diet Coke over Diet Pepsi just to get the excerpt? Only time will tell, for consumers are well-known to march to the beat of their own drum.

What's this all about?—*how money becomes wealth,* that's what!

Reading *The Wall Street Journal* is a course in Capitalism 101. It's an excellent and easy way to get comfortable with "putting four hotels on your property" without flinching. The No. 1 daily newspaper (circulation 1,837,194) is owned by the Dow Jones & Company, Inc., famous for the DJIA (Dow Jones Industrial Average) daily scoreboard—aka the folks providing comprehensive stock market reports. The history and development of the Dow Jones & Company is in itself an incredible story of sheer capitalism.

We all want our business know-how and portfolios to grow and grow, so the more we grasp, from lingo to concepts to politics to being visionaries, the more successful we will be. Try this piece on for size:

OMNICOM GAINS

Omnicom said net income for the third quarter rose 30% to $53.8 million, or 32 cents a diluted share, from the year-earlier $41.5 million, or 26 cents a diluted share. Revenue from commission and fee income increased 31% to $981.6 million from $746.8 million. Revenue outside the U.S. grew faster than domestic revenue, gaining 37% to $472.4 million, compared with a 27% increase in domestic revenue to $509.2 million.

At first you might respond with "Huh?" but then "Oh, I get it." You start to absorb and appreciate what you've read. We're honest women; we admit we love the sound and click and look of big figures and the word *million.* How about you?

CAPITALISTS-AT-THEIR-ZENITH

The thing about capitalism is there's the good, the bad, the ugly, and the politics. One almost unbelievable legend is re-played again and again, so you may as well have it under your belt.

The all-time story of capitalists-at-their-zenith, displaying all the elements of the good, the bad, the ugly, the politics, and an eat-all-you-want free lunch, is that of the infamous Big Four: Collis Huntington, Mark Hopkins, Leland Stanford, and Charles Crocker. The following is an extract from the book *The Wealthy 100* (which, we regret to say, does not list any women.)

Businessmen as well as politicians, the Big Four, originally from various states, landed and met in Sacramento, Califor-nia, during the Gold Rush. They, however, struck it rich in railroads, not gold. Their stake struck hold when Huntington introduced the group to an eccentric engineer named Theodore "Crazy Ted" Judah, the visionary of the Central Pa-cific Railroad. Judah had come up with a route to run a rail-road through the perilous California Sierra Nevada. But no bank would back him. The Big Four, with no experience in railroads, nevertheless gambled on Judah offering him a backing of $195,000, barely enough to start surveying. Sub-sequent lobbying by Huntington in Washington (greasing the wheels with bribes) led Congress to pass the Pacific Railway Act in 1862, bestowing the right to build the railroad from Sacramento to meet the Union Pacific railroad being built from the East. Huntington telegraphed Stanford: "We have drawn the elephant, now let us see if we can harness it."

The government paid for almost the whole project. The Big Four partners received $16,000 for every mile of track across flat land and $48,000 for every mile across the mountains. (When the federal government announced the mountain pay, Stanford quickly arranged for the state geologist to redraw the maps of the Sierra Nevada, adding an extra 24 miles to the width of the mountain range.) In addition, Stanford arranged for California to pay them $10,000 for every mile of track laid in the state. In all, the partners were given $25 million in government bonds and 4.5 million acres of land. Although the railroad was almost entirely financed by the government, the profits were kept by the partners.

Even before the Central Pacific was completed, through the virtual slavery of some 10,000 Chinese workers who chiseled through the mountains by hand for a $1 per day, the four men established the Southern Pacific, stretching from the West Coast to New Orleans. Along the route they built cities, becoming the largest landlords in California, Nevada, and Utah. In 1979, the magazine New West commented: "The hidden empire of Southern Pacific is so vast that it controls virtually every important area of policy and growth in California."

Huntington ended up the wealthiest, acquiring more railroads. Hopkins preferred the simple life. Stanford, a California governor, a U.S. Senator, and member of the Senate's Millionaires Club, is known best for founding one of the nation's most prominent universities—Stanford University at Palo Alto. Charles Crocker's estate developed the Crocker-Anglo National Bank.

The visionary Judah, questioning the tactics of his partners was eased out; his shares taken. He died penniless.

CAPITALISM WITHOUT A CONSCIENCE

Sometimes capitalism is like a runaway train. Someone makes a move—good, bad, or greedy—and things change instantly. A company trades in its people conscientiousness for the last buck. In 1986, for example, the Safeway Grocery chain was the victim of a leverged buyout by cash-rich corporate raiders. According to *Capitalist Fools* (another fascinating read): "Wholesale closings and firings followed, as the new Safeway transformed from a healthy, useful, and profitable social organization, into a desperate company struggling to pay its debts and stay alive."

This true story, of the Safeway closings and firings, and how it affected people's lives (suicides, heart attacks, unemployment, parentless children), was brought to the forefront by writer and author Susan Faludi. Her compassionate Pulitzer Prize winning story appeared on the front page of *The Wall Street Journal*.

The point: When powerful money lords—aka CEOs, Big Boys, Wall Street Studs—cry out "Buy this, sell that" without taking into consideration the human factor, injury to individuals can take a tremendous toll.

We hope women as millionaires will be different and know how to handle conglomerating and disconglomerating business, not people.

AIMING HIGHER

A contemporary visionary and leader working to make things better is writer and television producer Norman Lear of Stanford, California. He founded The Business Enterprise Trust, which honors companies or individuals who have shown breakthrough leadership in combining sound business management with social conscience. Featured in the book *Aiming Higher,* here are two companies run by women entrepreneurs who have done exceedingly well with this philosophy:

1. Freelance Photographers Guild (FPG) is a thriving business which acquires and sells photographs—some 7 million in 1996. Stock photography is simply the business of accumulating a wide variety of photographs that are sold to clients for advertising, illustrating books or magazine articles, greeting cards, marketing, and other commercial uses. For decades, stock photography tended to idealize white, affluent mainstream America, while virtually ignoring ethnic minorities, women on the job, the disabled, gays and lesbians, the elderly, and the gamut of social issues. FPG President Barbara Roberts felt a need to develop a new corporate culture based on cooperation, civility, and diversity. In 1995, she and Jessica Brackman, the 30-year-old daughter of FPG's founder, and the person who had hired Roberts, issued a Real Life Catalog, which grossed an amazing $500,000. With her social passions and ideals in guiding a series of management reforms, back-office computerization, and the cultivation of a new corporate culture, Roberts boosted revenues from $7 million to $35 million. Her company is now the second largest stock agency in the world.

2. Rachel's Bus Company, an inner-city Chicago-based business operating school busses, boasts $4.5 million in annual revenues, 23 full-time staff, and 140 part-time bus drivers. It was successfully developed by Rachel Hubka, who previously built a school-busing empire for a previous employer. When he decided to quit, Hubka mortgaged her home to the hilt to buy him out. As the new fleet owner, Rachel's biggest problem was finding an affordable location for her enterprise. She needed an immense garage, modest office space, and fuel pumps—all in a location with easy access to city expressways. She also needed to recruit and retain drivers. Rachel chose North Lawndale, one of Chicago's most depressed areas

with severe unemployment. Her philosophy: "I wanted to give the inner city people an opportunity to come in and work, where they may not have had opportunities in the past. I knew I had a training program to offer for men and women who hadn't had an opportunity to get the kind of training they need to get an income. The people here are interested in working. They need work, and I need employees."

Who is backing these new thinking business tactics? Lear's Business Enterprise Trust has some famous names on its Board of Trustees. For example, billionaire Warren E. Buffett of Berkshire Hathaway; Katharine Graham, The Washington Post Company; John T. Walton, Walton Family Foundation; Kay Koplivitz, USA Networks; and Karen N. Horn, Bank One. Another influential associate is journalist Bill Moyers, who narrates teaching videos produced by the Trust that are then distributed by Harvard Business School to some 450 educational and corporate training institutions.

Overall, most big businesses toe the line, setting both social and financial goals. They have to; their community services and good-guys images are good PR. From a set budget, they fund proposals, sponsor events, and make donations to fundraisers. Soft-headed business? Political correctness? Hardly. It's just good business sense to nurture the hand that feeds you.

Another issue is the capital, or loot, earned by CEOs of Fortune 500 companies. By law public companies are required to disclose the pay of their top five executives. So let's take advantage of *Hoover's Handbook of American Business* (1998):

- In San Francisco, discount brokerage Charles Schwab Corporation Chairman and CEO, Charles Schwab, age 60: $10,187,299
- In New York City, investment banking firm Salomon, Inc., Co-CEO Deryck C. Maughan, age 49: $9,420,000

- In Islandia, New York, and in California and in 43 foreign countries, Computer Associates Chairman and CEO, Charles B. Wang, age 52: $6,000,000

The room at the top is spellbinding. Here's Time-Warner's five-man lineup:

- Chairman and CEO Gerald M. Levine, age 57: $5,050,000
- SVC Robert E. "Ted" Turner III, age 58: $1,235,246
- President Richard D. Parsons, age 48: $2,900,000
- EVP, Secretary, and General Counsel Peter R. Hayes, age 62: $1,825,000
- SVP and CFO Richard J. Bressler, age 39: $1,425,000

Some women are earning hefty incomes as well. In January 1997, *Working Women* magazine listed the compensations of women executives, which includes base salary, stock awards, bonuses, and other compensation. Linda Wachner, 50, Chair, CEO, and President of Warnaco Group, is the highest paid executive, male or female, in the entire apparel industry with a total compensation package of $11 million. Carol Bartz, Chair, CEO, and President of Autodesk gets $5.51 million, while Sally Crawford, COO of Healthsource takes in $4.02 million. Sally Crawford is to be commended. In the early '80s, Crawford was working for a small, for-profit HMO working like a beast, in fact, for wages that barely covered her babysitter's costs. As she rose in the firm, it occured to her that her contributions were worth a big chunk of company stock. Nothing doing, her boss told her. "I left the company three weeks later," she says. "Equity participation is key to me."

Equity participation, or any other kind of participation in big business, is key to winning more of those million-dollar box seats that need gender parity. A good move is for more women to get on boards as directors; a better move is to get on as an insider (officers of a corporation who also serve on the board).

Women hold 671 board seats out of a total of 6,064, or 11.1 percent of Fortune 500 board seats. Of the Fortune 500 companies, 429 have women directors, and more than one-third, or 188 companies, boast multiple women directors, according to the 1998 Catalyst Census of Women Board Directors of the Fortune 500.

How can big business help you in your quest? Just remember that many big businesses had humble beginnings, had to persevere through many decades, and succeeded through the implementation of various strategies. General Mills got started after winning a gold medal for flour at an 1880 exposition. They quickly introduced Gold Medal Flour and created fictional spokeswoman Betty Crocker.

In the 1880s, book salesman David McConnel gave small bottles of perfume to New York housewives who listened to his sales pitch. The perfume was more popular than the books. Thus was born Avon. Avon has since branched into jewelry, apparel, gifts, home decorations, goal setting seminars for women, and toys. Avon's most successful product introduction ever? Winter Velvet Barbie.

In 1971, Charles Schwab, initially a full-service broker, moved into discount brokerage after the Securities and Exchange Commission outlawed fixed commissions in 1975. While most brokers defiantly raised commissions, Schwab cut its rates steeply.

Strategy, strategy, strategy.

EXERCISES

1. Go to a business library and give yourself a full tour. Study capitalism.

2. In the library reference department, review the wealth of information in each of the following: *Million Dollar Directory* from Dun & Bradstreet, *Reference Book of Corporate Management* from Dun & Bradstreet, *Standard Rate and Data* books for advertising information, *Thomas Register of American Manufacturers, Standard & Poor's Register of Corporations, Directors, and Executives, Enclopedia of Associations,* and *Standard Directory of Advertisers.*

3. It's easier to conduct business when you know how to talk business. Buy a business dictionary and learn the language.

4. Call your local convention center and inquire about big business conventions. Attend or volunteer to work at one or two.

5. Read the individual stories of the Fortune 500.

6. Check out your governments—city, county, state, and federal—for contract awards. Ask about their bidding process. Get on their mailing lists.

7. Pick the companies you're interested in and send for their annual reports. Learn how to read them.

8. Check your local universities' schools of business for affiliations. Ask for their alumni lists. You never know who might be on those lists that can help you with your enterprise.

Write an Unbeatable Business Plan

Twenty-seven-year-old entrepreneur Christy Haubegger was chosen as one of the top ten role models of 1997 by the Ms. Foundation for Women. In addition, she was named one of the most inspirational women of 1996 by *NBC Nightly News with Tom Brokaw* and has been lauded in *Crain's New York Business* as one of the youngest business women in the United States. She's also been profiled in *MediaWeek, Glamour, Ms., Cosmopolitan, Los Angeles Times,* on CNN and ABC, and countless other print and broadcast media.

Who is Christy Haubegger? She is President of Latina Publications, LLC, and publisher of *Latina* magazine, which she launched in May 1996 with an unbeatable business plan financed by Ed Lewis, CEO of *Essence Magazine!*

A BUSINESS PLAN IS A MAP

Let's clarify. A business plan is a written document from 10 to 30 pages or more with two main purposes: (1) to raise money and (2) to prepare an operating plan.

Some folks believe the business plan is the first thing you do when you say you're going to start a business. On the other hand, those of us who have their start-ups on our kitchen tables or in the corner of our bedrooms generally won't write a formal business plan until we're ready to launch into a bigger market, if at all.

Christy's vision, however, was big right from the beginning. Rather than starting off with a newsletter that could later grow into a magazine, she went for the whole enchilada. She began by researching and talking to the titans of publishing. She researched her target market very thoroughly. She kept careful notes, recording interviews and gathering statistics, until she had sufficient information to begin writing.

Once her file folders were bulging with data, she organized an accurate and enticing business plan. Here are the types of information she gathered:

- Executive summary
- Product and market information
- Activities to date
- Strengths and weaknesses
- Company operations
- Management team
- Funding requirements
- Business pro forma
- Action time line
- Formal offer

THE EXECUTIVE SUMMARY IS KEY

The executive summary is perhaps the most important segment of any plan because it's the first page a potential investor reads. In writing articles or books, for example, writers know they have to *hook the reader* in the first lines. The same holds true with the executive summary—you want to *hook the investor* quickly.

The executive summary is challenging because it needs to be short and sweet—no more than two to three pages—but has a lot to tell. It needs to include:

- What you're doing (e.g., introducing product/service *X*)
- What your sales proposition is (who will buy your product/service and why)
- Why you feel your product/service will be successful (e.g., you surveyed, you tested your product/service, you sold $*X* worth/*X* number of units, or you have a growth projection)
- Why you need the money (e.g., to start, to expand, to develop, to manufacture, to market, to become a millionaire)
- How much money you need
- How much money you are investing (Are you confident enough to risk your own cash?)
- Your expected sales (e.g., you expect initial sales of $1 million to grow into $10 million within *X* amount of time)

Sometimes the executive summary is your only shot at presenting your case. Bettina, for example, sought money for a worldwide infomercial for the Spanish version of her book. However, when she found an interested investor, all he wanted to see was the executive summary. So, back to the writing board she went. If that was her only shot, she figured it had better be powerful and persuasive. Unfortunately, although the initial investor liked her idea, a decision-making committee didn't buy her plan. Bettina feels she did well with the initial investor because she "pitched to him over the telephone." She didn't get that opportunity with the other committee members. Something to remember.

Of course, the executive summary is a summary, it can only come into being after the entire plan has been written. This means it is essential to invest some time, energy, and passion into developing a professional looking, convincing business plan.

Convincing is key. Investors, God bless them, look for and rate specifics. Are you a prudent money manager? Do you have a sound management team? How much money do you, yourself, plan to invest? (The hard truth, you need money to raise money.) And the all-important elements—are the basic operations of your company-to-be well thought out, documented, and proven?

YOUR MANAGEMENT TEAM

The management team is simply a collection of brief resumés of the people who will be working with you in operations as well as in advisory positions (i.e., your board). Investors look for expertise and credentials, as well as wisdom and commitment. Obviously, if the management team isn't sound no one will invest.

When Christy Haubegger was seeking investors, she teamed up with Sandra Guzman, who is now *Latina*'s editor-in-chief. Haubegger, an attorney, graduated from the University of Texas at Austin and Stanford Law School, where she was president of her class. Guzman, a graduate of Rutgers University, is a well-respected, award-winning journalist who lists the prestigious

Emmy award given by the New York Chapter of the National Academy of Television Arts and Sciences among her many honors.

A credible team with excellent credentials!

WRITING YOUR BUSINESS PLAN

Writing, of course, doesn't come easily for everyone and a business plan compounded with details must be clear. Nonetheless, it can be done when your passion for whatever it is you're burning to do burns from the first page to the last.

So study books, get help from experienced folks, take a class, and expect to do multiple rewrites. Diane Jacobs, owner of The Cakeworks, in Los Angeles, California, recalls getting seven books on business plans from the library. "I wanted to learn all the different perspectives," she says.

An irony: You need money to raise money. Backing your plan of action with money of your own is commonly required. Take, for example, Lavonne Luquis, recipient of the 1998 Hispanic Achievement Award. In 1995, Lavonne confesses, she didn't know how to finance a start-up. She'd never sold an advertisement, let alone a Web ad. And she'd never heard of an IPO (initial public offering). "I didn't know diddly-squat," said Luquis. "But I didn't know I didn't know diddly-squat."

Nevertheless, Lavonne developed her LatinoLink Web site from savings, a business loan, and $5,000 in credit card debt. While her associate Max Ramirez was keeping the computers running, Luquis went out and sold ads to keep LaintoLink running on the World Wide Web. She didn't target purely Hispanic sponsors, either. The site's first advertiser was brokerage giant Charles Schwab. Current advertisers include AT&T, IBM, and Microsoft. In late 1998, LatinoLink made headlines when it was one of 21 Internet companies Zapata Inc. invested in or bought outright. (Alas, business is fickle, Zapata cancelled all of these deals months later.)

As an aside for all millionairesses-to-be, and relating to marketing, the Hispanic population is not something you want to ignore. "It is like a tidal wave coming at us," says Michael Bevan, Toyota Corp's U.S. advertising manager. The Latino count as a whole has reached 30 million, about 11 percent of the total U.S. population, according to census data. And Latinos already have a purchasing power of $348 billion.

Interestingly, Christy Haubegger was born to a Mexican-American mother, but adopted by a German couple. Her adoptive parents insisted she keep her culture alive. She is seeing the big payoff.

The first issue of *Latina* hit the newsstands in June 1996. Before the year ended, the magazine had gone from quarterly to bimonthly. The *monthly* milestone hit in 1997. *Latina*'s circulation of 175,000 challenges the more established *People Espanol* at 200,000 and is dusting *Estilo* at 75,000 and *Glamour en Espanol* at 65,000.

BUSINESS PLANS FOR ESTABLISHED BUSINESSES

Business plans are also valuable as in transitional *bail-out* tools. Take Patty DeDominic's company PDQ Personnel Services that places workers in temporary jobs. She'd been in business for four years when she realized a growth spurt month meant she wouldn't be able to make her payroll. When she gathered her employees and explained the situation, one immediately came forward with a $5,000 check as a loan. Better yet, one woman staffer was married to an investment banker, another to a CPA. Those two professionals helped DeDominic work out a business plan she could take to her banker. With it, she secured a $25,000 line of credit—enough to keep the business afloat.

That was in 1983. PDQ now has a revenue of about $20 million, a staff of about 40, and 760 or so temporary workers on payroll. Patty plans to expand nationwide. A sensitive woman, who started PDQ after working as an operations manager for another placement agency, Patty treats her employees like gold. She provides them training with pay, volunteerism with pay, flex time, and profit sharing to the tune of 10 percent.

THE BOTTOM LINE

Growth and profit must always be your goal, and spelling out your plan to achieve it is the whole reason for your business plan. If you are starting a new business, you must have a clear understanding of the potential market as well as all the possible potholes in your path.

If you aim to take your business to the next step through expansion or wider distribution, you must clearly demonstrate to potential investors or lenders that your added expenses will be easily offset by increased income. Too much, too fast is one of the main reasons new businesses fail. Be sure each stage of your business plan is substantiated with accurate figures based on conservative expectations. No pie in the sky here. Instead, expect calamities. Budget sufficient resources to replace your air-conditioning system in mid-August or your furnace in February, or to cover unexpected costs due to a strike affecting a major supplier or your spending six weeks in traction in a hospital.

Remember, investors and lenders need more than enthusiasm. They need your clear route to profit and growth. And the map that will demonstrate that route is your unbeatable business plan.

EXERCISES

1. Before you start your unbeatable business plan, collect business loan applications from a variety of financial institutions—banks, commercial finance companies, and government agencies. Study them. Analyze the type of information they request.

2. Assess your own self-worth. Determine how much cash you can bring into your project.

3. Make a list of family members who have disposable income and who you think will loan you money. Write out or outline your approach per each person's value system. Rehearse it. Be ready with a promissory note.

4. Repeat 3 with a list of friends.

5. Start developing your executive summary *hook sentence;* dream on it.

6. Don't sweat the writing. If you don't write, hire someone who does. Don't sweat the formatting. If you don't know how, hire someone who does.

7. Research, research, research. Whatever your plan is, be sure you have it well supported with statistics, illustrations, examples, and comparisons.

8. Complete it.

9. Present. Mail. Call. Follow up. Network. Climb over every mountain. And refuse to let obstacles get in your way.

10. The name of the game in an unbeatable business plan? Growth and profit.

LESSON 14

Learn to Ask, Ask, and Ask for Money Again and Again

If your goal is to get big fast, then you'll need to polish your business plan, practice your sales pitch loud and clear, shoot the dice, pass go, and land on either California's Silicon Valley or New York's Silicon Alley for angel or venture capital.

Everyone knows New York City and everyone should know the Silicon Valley, the high-tech mecca where millionaires are born. This California hot spot, a 50-mile stretch between San Jose and San Francisco produces millionaires like a cash crop.

According to Payment Systems, Inc., in 1994 there were 45,000 millionaires in Silicon Valley; in 1996, there were 186,511! More specifically, in the same year, a Valley company went public every five days, minting 62 new millionaires every day! "Even the receptionists are millionaires," wrote Linda Himelstein in *Business Week*. (See that incredible story in Lesson 17.)

And lots of those millionaires and millionaire companies got off the ground because of angel and venture capital.

MONEY FROM ANGELS

There is a distinction between angels and venture capital. The term *angel* was coined decades ago on New York City's Broadway. It was designed to lure wealthy people who invested in theatrical productions, as in, "You're an angel, dahling!"

Angels are simply cash-rich folks who invest, hoping eventually to earn a big return somewhere down the line—maybe as much as 40 percent—but knowing they may lose it all. The U.S. Small Business Administration estimated that 250,000 angels are active in the country, funneling capital into 30,000 small companies a year, for a total investment of $20 billion. That's twice what the professional venture-capital industry invested in its record year of 1996.

Investments for angels usually start around $10,000, are often informal, and may be risky. Angels may band together to help a fledgling company meet, say, a $1 million goal. For example, in 1996, 12 of the 100 members of The Band of Angels, a group in the Silicon Valley, invested $1.2 million in Dina Britton, a computer scientist and founder of software start-up DBStar.

Angels are frequently active investors who want to get up close and personal with their companies, to monitor progress and even act as advisers. They sometimes sit on boards of the companies they fund. While some groups of angels focus only on high-tech investments, The Gathering of Angels in New Mexico considers funding everything from retailers to restaurants and software and biotechnology companies.

Amazon.com, the Internet bookseller, is the perhaps the most famous company that benefited from angel investment. In 1994, Jeff Bezos and a few employees created the firm's Web site and database in Bezos' Bellevue, Washington, garage. Bezos then went looking for private investors because no venture capitalists were interested in the company at that point. He succeeded in raising $1.2 million from about a dozen angels. A year later, $8 million in professional venture capital followed. Go, Jeff!

Silicon Alley (adapted from Silicon Valley) is the ambitious nickname for New York's concentration of new-media businesses. There, the New York Angel Investor Program in Manhattan is one of many agencies who funnel money from private capital to entrepreneurs.

VENTURE CAPITAL

Professional venture firms generally won't even look at a business that needs less than $2 million. Their investment is based on careful review of a company's business plan and accomplishments to date. Investments are made only when a good return is virtually guaranteed, and is often in exchange for a percentage of the company. By the time a company goes public, the venture capitalists may own up to 80 percent of it. Big time operators are sometimes referred to as *vulture capitalists.*

Two famous women, Marleen McDaniel and Ellen Pack of Wire Networks, Inc., raised $7 million from venture capitalists to launch the largest Web site targeted to women. Their path to their online magazine wasn't easy. "It's absolutely more difficult for women to raise venture capital," declares president and CEO McDaniel. Between 1991 and 1996, women only got 1.6 percent of the $35 billion in venture capital invested in high tech.

Still, the more women do this—the more we go knocking on the doors of angels, venture capitalists, any capitalists in sight— the more likely the doors to the money vaults will open for us. The doors swung wide for successful high-tech venture capital finders Cheryl Vedoe of Tenth Planet Explorations ($15 million) and Katrina Garnett of Crossroads, Inc. ($1 million). Way to go!

And then there's Lisa Argiris of International Musical Suppliers. "All the banks were interested in me," says Argiris, 34, "[but they were] astonishingly poor at offering me what I needed and were looking instead at what they were comfortable doing." The sticking point for the banks was the structure of the deal. Instead of settling for less, however, Lisa persevered and after 16 weeks of searching she landed a $1.5 million loan—on her own terms.

If you happen to be on the West Coast, and you're ready to make your pitch, get ready for dinner at the ritzy Los Altos Country Club in the foothills of the Silicon Valley. On the second or third Wednesday of each month about 50 millionaires from the Board of Angels eat, drink, and catch up on the latest, then listen to presentations from start-up companies. The catch? You have to be invited by a member. That's right—more butt-breaking behavior is required.

Oh, and if you can't make that affair you can always try attending one of the venture capital fairs popping up nationwide. Many cities have either formal or informal groups interested in fostering local entrepreneurs and fledgling businesses. These fairs are attended by individual investors as well as early-stage venture capitalists and give you a target-rich environment in which to pitch your wares. For example, a fair known as Early Stage East was held in June 1998 in Wilmington, Delaware. The fair attracted 180 investors to rub elbows with 24 entrepreneurs on hand to share their stories and convince investors that their companies would return a multiple of the investment in a very short time.

MONEY IS EVERYWHERE— ASK AND ASK AGAIN

There is no shortage of money. Here's a partial list of potential sources of capital:

- borrowing,
- debt financing (loan/borrowing),
- subordinated debt (see your accountant),
- commercial banks,
- commercial finance companies,
- leasing companies,
- savings and loan associations,
- the Small Business Administration,
- industrial revenue bonds,
- life insurance companies and pension funds,
- leveraged buyouts,
- research and development partnerships,
- small business investments companies,
- minority enterprise small business investment companies,
- small business innovation research grants and, of course,
- friends, family members, or anyone who believes in you enough to lend you $$$$$.

A famous saying goes: "Businesses don't fail. They just run out of money." And it's a fact of life that for the business person, raising money is a way of life. It goes on and on. And because it does, you must be resourceful and persistent. But here's a hint: Do not overlook a combination of financing.

Another way, today, to raise money for an established company is to *go public*. This simply means to offer stock through an initial public offering, or an IPO. It is, however, a complex, costly undertaking (in the hundreds of thousands of dollars). Still, the mere mention of IPO leaves most of us starry-eyed, lusting for the rewards.

Successful IPOs have made folks into instant-aires over and over. Think-and-prep time for an IPO is said to be one to three years. Then it's all about national and worldwide economic trends and, most importantly, timing.

The lesson here? If you are considering an IPO, do your homework. Lots of it. Study, research, network, find a peer who has been through it, ask away, and then ask some more. Here's an example of an attempt to go public with someone most of us recognize.

> Donna Karan, 48
> Chairman of the board, CEO and chief designer, Donna Karan International.
> 1996 net revenue: $612.8 million
> Stake: Owns 24.7 percent of company with husband
> Education: Parsons School of Design
> Per *Success,* Donna Karan's empire started with ready-to-wear women's fashions and men's clothes. Then it was on to beauty products and fragrances and, most recently, candles and pillows.
> Karan began with two years' study at Parsons, then became assistant to fashion star Anne Klein. When Klein died, Karan became her successor, creating the Anne Klein II collection, then starting her own business in 1984.
> Today she has 1,600 employees, whom she says she views as an extended family. "That I'm a woman makes me want to nurture others, fulfill needs, and solve problems," she says.
> Karan planned an IPO in 1993 but withdrew it because of disappointing sales. When she finally took the company public in 1996, shares initially rose—then plummeted sharply. Ah well, the business world is tough.

HIS MONEY, YOUR MONEY, OUR MONEY—
WHATEVER IT TAKES

Hey, if you don't need to leave the house, then don't. If your husband or parents will lend you money, why do it the hard way? In 1991, for example, Michele McCormick of Folsom, California, wrote a business plan that called for $20,000 to open

MMC Communications, her public relations firm in Sacramento. She had $10,000 and the rest came in an interest-free $10,000 loan from her husband.

"I paid it back in dribs and drabs," she says, "and it took me probably two years. I was making an income, but of course I wasn't making money until I'd reached the $20,000 mark of the original investment." In 1998, MMC billed approximately $400,000.

Sometimes just the opposite happens—a wife loans the money to her husband's business. *Essence* magazine tells the story of Sheila Crup Johnson, 49, the executive vice-president of Corporate Affairs for BET Holdings, Inc. in Washington, D.C. Her estimated net worth: $210 million. In 1979, Sheila cosigned a $15,000 loan so her husband, Robert, could quit his job and launch Black Entertainment Television (BET), the first black-owned company listed on the New York Stock Exchange. Valued at about $1 billion, BET is now privately held, with Robert owning 65 percent.

MEET A WOMAN WITH THE CLOUT TO HAND DOUGH OUT

In 1997, Aida Alvarez was appointed the new administrator of the Small Business Administration (SBA). Her job is to spread opportunities by making loans easier for folks who generally can't meet the *cookie cutter* criteria of traditional lending institutions.

One of her goals is to support the entrepreneurial earthquake of women wanting to go into business for themselves by creating more programs. When asked what she could do for women who have poor credit due to divorces or other circumstances, Alvarez replied, "The SBA is working on that too."

The SBA is a lender of last resort. You must be turned down by other lenders to qualify for an SBA loan. The SBA doesn't lend money directly to you; instead, it guarantees 80 percent of a bank's loan up to $100,000 and 75 percent on loans over $100,000.

The main advantage of SBA is their long repayment schedule—from 10 to 25 years—which makes terms affordable. Another advantage is that the approval of credit is based, at least in part, on the character of the applicant and does not require full collateral coverage. Rates are reasonable, but programs are subject to government funding being available. They also have a lot of restrictions and require a lot of paper processing. Recently, the SBA began a woman's funding program.

Apart from being a source of financing, the SBA is a source for women interested or starting out or wanting to develop their skills. They can draw on any of the 60 SBA-supported women's development centers from Anchorage, Alaska, to San Juan, Puerto Rico.

SCROLLING, BROWSING, AND DIALING FOR DOLLARS

American Express is just going to have to drop their archaic "Don't leave home without out it" slogan, because in these high-tech days you don't even have to leave home or your office for much of anything—it's all on the Internet. And when it comes to finding money, clicking gets you there in a matter of seconds, with packaged offerings ever so tempting.

One site, for example, www.cashfinder.com enables a small-business owner to be matched with the most appropriate lender after answering a few questions. If you need expansion capital, consider the Women's Growth Capital Fund in Washington, D.C. It's the largest fund of its kind and the first women-licensed Small Business Investment Company (SBIC). Just go to www. womensgrowth.com.

We can't close this section without mentioning yet another Internet phenomenon—launching an IPO online! In 1995, attorney and beermaker (WIT ales) Andrew Klein was the first entrepreneur to conduct an online IPO and he raised $1.6 million for his New York City business. In a 1998 interview with *Nations Business,* Klein said, "I do think that you're going to see increasing opportunities, like the opportunity that my beer company had to raise venture capital from patient investors—angel investors and other investors—through the Internet."

EXERCISES

1. Ask, ask, and ask for money again and again.

2. Call your local chamber of commerce and inquire about venture fairs. Attend at least one just to see how it works. Plan what you would do to keep all investors' eyes and ears on you and how you would beat the competition.

3. For your money hunt, write a go-for-the-gold list, that is, a list that constitutes a good match between your idea/ product/service/business and investors.

4. Read *Where to Go When the Bank Says No: Alternatives for Financing Your Business* by David R. Evanson.

5. Participate in a venture fair. Get a booth, have great handouts, make a presentation.

6. Catch the television show *Money Hunt* on your local PBS station. For broadcast times visit: www.moneyhunter.com/ htm/show/times/htm.

7. Join your local chamber of commerce.

8. Check out these Web sites:
   - Trade Show News Network at www.entrepreneurmag.com
   - ACE-Net Angel Capital Electronic Network, sponsored by the SBA Office of Advocacy at www/sba.gov. Click on financing and ACE-Net
   - PriCap (Private Capital Clearinghouse) NVST at www.nvst.com
   - America's Business Funding Directory at www.businessfinance.com
   - OTInetwork, The Online Technology Investment Network at www.otnetwork.com
   - FinanceHub at www.financehub.com

Don't Be Shy—
Build a High Profile
for Success

What is the surest way to rocket yourself to the top of both your career and your finances? Stand up and be noticed! Build yourself a high profile and make sure that everyone around you knows that you are headed for big things.

What is a high profile? A high profile means that *you* are the first person that comes to mind in many situations. A woman with a high profile is the one who is called into meetings for a last minute opinion, the one who comes back from lunch to find a message from a television reporter who wants to schedule an interview, the one whose letters to the editor actually get printed, the one who is asked to join the board of the bank.

A woman with a high profile can translate that image into increased career opportunities—and increased salary opportunities. A woman with a high profile can translate that image into more clients, more business, and more opportunity to see her business income grow!

A woman with a high profile has created an aura of success and achievement around herself. And, once established, that aura of success will just continue to grow and grow.

Sounds great! But how do you go about building a high profile? Doesn't it just happen to a lucky few, the ones who look like movie stars and have perfect hairdos? No. High profiles happen to women who intentionally go out and seek them.

Let's look at an example of an extremely high-profile person— Donald Trump. Is he the richest builder in New York City? No. Is he the most successful person in New York City? No. Is he the best dealmaker in New York City? No. Was he *ever* any of those things? Nope.

But despite all that, he has positioned himself that way in the minds of millions of people. How? By using the media, he built himself the image that he wanted to project. The aura of success and invincibility.

And when his empire crashed, when he was hundreds of millions of dollars in debt, his high-profile image really paid off. Because he was *still* able to borrow money from banks. He was *still* able to put real estate deals together. He was *still* able to attract media attention.

BE PERSISTENTLY RELENTLESS

We hear so much about PR nowadays—public relations. And yes, public relations is a big part of building a high profile, but we like to interpret PR a whole different way. Start thinking of PR as *persistently relentless!* Not only should you be persistently relentless in your pursuit of that profitable high-profile image, but in any area of your life where you want to succeed. Success happens to those who seek it out and don't give up at the very first set back. Persist!

Here is how you can be persistently relentless while building up your public image:

- *First, familiarize yourself with the media in your area.* Learn who writes for the local paper and what areas they cover. Start to pay attention to the *bylines,* the name of the person who has written the story. Learn who books guests onto the local television talk shows. Sound hard? It couldn't be easier, just pick up the phone, call the station and ask!
- *Next, introduce yourself to these folks.* Write a letter commenting on a recent article that they wrote, or story that was aired on television. Mention your own interest or connection to the topic ("I, too, am a human resources professional . . ."). And compliment them on a job well done. Don't try to sell yourself in this first contact.
- *Then, work to be included in stories.* Wait a few weeks after your first letter, and then follow up in writing with a unique story idea. In this second letter you can mention yourself as a suitable expert source, or possible interviewee.

Why would they want to talk to you? Don't forget that 24 hours a day media outlets need something to talk about, something to report on, something to broadcast. And if you can come to them with a solid idea, you are helping them do their jobs and fill that space!

Once you have gained a certain level of profile in your area, you are ready to branch out on a larger scale. It's time to tackle the national media! Put together a file of the articles that have been written about you, or the articles in which you are mentioned. Tailor your message for a national (instead of a regional) audience, and start pitching yourself to the national media!

Jennifer: I'm just a small town girl from Sacramento, but over the years I've been mentioned or featured in newspapers like the Boston Globe, LA Times, New York Post *and* Chicago

Tribune. *And television shows like* American Journal—*they did a ten minute segment on me that ran right after a segment on Arnold Schwarzenegger! So never let your idea (or worse yet, your family's idea) of who you are hold you back.*

Bettina: While publicizing my first book, Chiquita's Cocoon, *I was really daring. I went down to the local newspaper dressed in a costume and ended up with not just a small article, but a full page article—with a half page picture of me and my book! You have to be daring, it really pays off.*

Become a real student of national media, too. Study the articles in *People,* or *Working Woman,* or wherever you want to be featured. Why do they choose the topics they choose? Who are these people and what have they done? And how can you position yourself like that?

Is there a way to get media folks to call you instead? Yes. A publication called *Radio and Television Interview Report* will happily sell you an ad in their monthly editions or their annual book of experts. This magazine is sent to radio and television producers across the country who comb through it looking for interesting guests (remember, that is their job!). You can simply buy an ad that advertises your availability as an expert talk show guest on a particular topic. And it only costs a few hundred dollars! For details, call 800-989-1400.

CREATE SOMETHING SPECIAL

Don't think there is anything special about who you are and what you do? Then get to work and *create something special.*

Here is what real estate agent Margaret Greenberg did in order to separate herself from the pack of other folks selling houses: "There were so many real estate agents working the same area of town that I specialized in, I knew that as the newest and youngest I'd get lost in the pack. So I created a free neighborhood newsletter filled with articles about interesting things to do and local issues. Of course, I included information on myself and my real estate business in every issue, but it was a real soft sell. I developed quite a reputation in the neighborhood as someone who really cared about what went on there. And it worked—I did get clients as a result!"

So don't just sit there—create something! Can you create a newsletter or a public access cable television show, write a book, organize a community event, or develop an organization that you can use to further broadcast your own talents, business, or career?

Once you really embrace the idea that a high profile is what you desire, become a student of public relations. If you invest the time in honing your skills, you will be that much more successful in getting coverage. Here are just a few things to get you started:

- Learn to write press releases.
- Learn to hold a press conference.
- Join a speaking organization to polish your presentation and skills.
- Seek out media training; learn how to be an effective radio or television guest.
- Have professional photos taken of yourself in a business setting.

And just how is all of this going to help you on the road to wealth and career success? Because it positions *you* as the woman that everyone wants.

Think about it—who gets hired? The woman with the good reputation. Who gets paid a bunch of money? The woman whose high profile creates an image of success. Who gets a bank loan? The woman that the bank officer reads about in the business magazine. And who gets asked to be a partner in a new venture? The woman that was on television last week.

So what do you want your high profile to be about? You need to decide just what you want to be well known for. Spend some time deciding. Your public message needs to be crafted in such a way that it not only appeals to people (and doesn't turn them off) but also creates a long-term benefit to your career. And it needs to be short, too.

You need what marketing folks call an *elevator speech*. Picture this: You're waiting for the elevator. It arrives and the doors slowly open to reveal that the only other occupant is the very important person you've been trying to get a meeting with for months! And here is your chance to have this person all to yourself for the next 30 seconds. Quick—what are you going to say?

> *Jennifer: I learned how to hone my elevator speech from one of the masters—a fellow named Bernard Zick. He helped me see just what it was that I wanted to create my public profile around, the theme that would best help build my career. If I ever have the great good fortune to share an elevator with a reporter from* The Wall Street Journal, *I'll stick out my hand and here's what I'll say: 'Hi there. I'm Jennifer Basye Sander, book packager. I create best-selling book ideas for myself and my clients.' Seems simple, but it took me the better part of an afternoon to get that focused!*

Think of it as a personal slogan of sorts. Just like Coke is "the real thing," you need to be something short and fast to help position yourself in the minds of the media when you are trying to pitch yourself. Not only will your personal slogan help you position yourself to the media, but it might also be a good launching pad for the creation of a public speaking career. With the help of her slogan, Jennifer speaks to writers groups on "How to Develop a Best-Selling Book Idea."

Bettina's elevator speech goes like this: "Hello. I'm Bettina Flores. I'm an author and seminar leader. I'm in the change business—I help women change their lives for the better. I just happen to have my book with me." (Of course, the book has a brochure and business card inside.)

Now with *The Millionairess Across the Street* at her side, Bettina is developing a new seminar: How to Develop a Million-Dollar Personality. This is not only a logical and natural sequence; it's an important issue for women in that personality is a human tool, a human factor that influences people from day to day. Women need to maximize their personalities to help achieve their goals. The more we open up to change, the more we get unstuck, the more we succeed.

Hone your message. Make it catchy, short, and sweet. Make it meaningful. Don't be shy. Get out there in front of a crowd and act as though you've always belonged. They will remember you and your business. They will remember you and your message! And as a result, you will prosper and flourish in many, many ways.

EXERCISES

1. Draw up a list of ideas for newspaper articles in which you could be featured. Create imaginary headlines for the articles about yourself.

2. Study an issue of *People* very carefully (no, not the movie star pieces, just the articles about regular folks). Draw up a list of imaginary articles for this magazine, too.

3. Brainstorm ideas for an organization that you can start (and run!). Running an organization is a great way to find yourself in the spotlight.

4. Learn all you can about writing press releases and getting free publicity. We recommend the book *Six Steps to Free Publicity* by Marcia Yudkin.

Don't Give It Away for Free—At Least Not All the Time

In September 1998, Joan Kroc, widow of Ray Kroc who built McDonald's into a fast-food super power, served up $80 million to the Salvation Army in San Diego. It was the largest single donation in the agency's history. Still, while it was extraordinary, Joan Kroc's generosity wasn't surprising. Earlier in the year, *Fortune* had named her the 36th most generous American based on her contributions to a number of organizations.

Joan Kroc is a billionaire. So wealthy that her donation barely makes a blip in her pocketbook. Unfortunately, too many of us emulate her, giving generously even when it affects our lifestyle.

WOMEN PUT THEMSELVES SECOND

Why are women so inclined to share, give, and lavish things on other people? "It's the way women are raised," declares Olivia Mellan, a Washington, D.C., speaker and author who specializes in the psychology of money. Her books, *Overcoming Overspending: A Winning Plan for Spenders and Their Partners* and *Money Harmony: Resolving Money Conflict in Your Life and Your Relationship,* delve into women's money-handling hang-ups.

Mellan, who is also a psychotherapist and business consultant in the area of financial-conflict resolution, deals with the emotional roots of money issues. She traces much of it to women's upbringing. "The messages women received as we grow up are: I'm not supposed to put myself first. I'm supposed to take care of everyone else first. The feminine value is to be accommodating, not competitive."

Women are just not used to being healthily self-oriented, she explains. "Think how many women put their husbands through college, and their kids in private schools," she continues. "Then they end up in a financial disaster as widows or divorcees, totally unprepared.

On a smaller scale, look at everyday life. Who takes the burnt toast? The broken taco? The chair with a not-so-good view of the TV set? Right. You do. Admit it. Even today, you wouldn't serve yourself the slightly larger brownie, whether you're with your father or your husband or your sister. It's not polite.

Men, of course, have little hesitation about taking the large piece. In our society, it's OK for men to put themselves first and acquire things, while women's usual habit is to give things away, to give themselves away.

MONEY AND YOUR CHILDREN

"I have to lecture parents about giving money to kids," laments Elfrena Foord, a Certified Financial Planner and a principal with Foord, VanBruggen & Ebersold, a Sacramento, California, financial planning and investment management firm. "I ask the parents, 'Do you think you're rich?'"

Now Foord isn't talking about money for a new bike or a couple special CDs for a child. She means substantial sums given to adult children. Sometimes, of course, gifts are appropriate and affordable. All too often, however, women—especially those who come into major money such as hitting it big at work, a lottery winning, or inheritance—give more than is prudent. Foord sees two reasons for big handouts.

The first she labels the ignorance factor. If they lack experience with large sums, they may forget about income taxes. They may not realize they may have to pay gift taxes on their children's behalf. "The parents haven't planned their own financial future," she says. "They haven't run the numbers about what it takes to be secure when you're 65 or 75 or 85. They just know that right now they have more money than their kids."

The second factor, Foord says, is that the parents haven't emancipated their kids. Parents sometimes forget the satisfaction of making it on your own. They want their kids to have it easier than they did. They forget it's time for their children to take care of themselves.

MONEY AND YOUR PARTNER

When a woman earns or inherits a lot of money, it can be hard on her relationship with her partner, Foord observes. There are questions to be settled. How much should you share? How much do you keep separate? How do you decide?

"It's something you have to work out," she says, noting that it is especially hard when a woman earns more than a male partner. "There are lots of male/female issues with money," she continues. She cites a client who recently divorced, primarily because her husband couldn't stand her earning a lot more than he did.

In some cases, Foord notes, "Having a lot of money could be so threatening to the relationship, the woman would do stupid things with her money." There are always options, Foord points out. You can keep your money separate. You can pay for special things. You can put it all in the same pot. It all depends on you and your partner.

It needs to be said, though, in this day and age, a woman must provide for herself. She needs to have her own pot of money, her *just in case* nest egg, her cookie or jam jar money, and her millionairess account.

MONEY AND CHARITIES

America has one of the highest rates of philanthropy in the world and American charities do many good works. Unfortunately, while there are many worthy organizations, there are also groups who prey on generous people. One elderly woman mailed thousands of dollars worth of small checks, mostly to dubious charities that obviously sold or swapped her name for their lists. Her daughter finally had to stop the woman's mail delivery; she was receiving six or more cunningly written appeals every day.

So give, but give wisely. If a charitable appeal arrives *bulk mail* rather than *nonprofit* notation, it's a red flag that the largest portion of their income probably goes to salaries and fundraising rather than their *worthy cause*. Ask questions. Where is my donation going? What percentage of your fundraising efforts simply support fundraising instead of the ultimate recipients? May I see your charity's financial statement for the last year?

Here are some other recommendations:

- Think globally, act locally. This means keep your charitable contributions in your own community by supporting local organizations whose work you admire.
- Contribute to your religious group.
- Donate only what you can afford while still protecting your financial plan.
- Budget your donations on an annual basis and don't exceed that amount.
- Give gifts of time and service rather than cash.

CHARITABLE PLEADINGS TO BUSINESSPEOPLE

Except for extremely low-key enterprises, businesspeople are the target of constant entreaties. Please, please, please sponsor our youth sports team, donate a prize for our church/school/youth/community raffle, do some free printing/transporting/catering to help fight cancer/illiteracy/poverty.

These pleas are all too familiar to Michele McCormick, founder of MMC, a public relations firm in Sacramento, California. She is often asked to donate her public relations expertise to worthy causes. "In my business," says McCormick, "all I have to sell is time and that's a very limited commodity." Sometimes she says yes. "It certainly is my instinct to want to get involved in issues and organizations that I believe have strong merit," she says. She's a past president of the Sacramento League of Women Voters, a member of the county parks commission, and a board member of the Sacramento Emergency Housing Center.

At the same time, she chooses commitments that also offer the chance for professional development or exposure to community leaders. In the past, such service has led to contacts that help her better serve her clients. "The personal satisfaction I get is important to the balance in my life," she says. "The added value is that I believe that balance enhances my professional capability as well."

For every *yes,* however, she says *no* at least five times. How? "It's not always easy," she concedes, "but I generally explain that I'm involved in several things, and it wouldn't be fair to take the place of someone who might give more time or focus. People are generally very understanding about that, especially because they are usually aware of my other activities."

BECOME SELF-ORIENTED

So what's the bottom-line solution to not giving it away for free? "Be sure your tendency to not put yourself first, doesn't put you in a precarious financial position," urges money expert Mellan.

Instead of being completely *other-oriented,* become *self-oriented*. Put yourself first. "Oh no," you protest, "I don't want to be selfish." But try saying it differently. Instead of *selfish,* use the term *self-caring*. This simply means taking care of yourself at least as well as you take care of everyone else.

Olivia Mellan offers the following advice on how to be a self-caring woman:

- Even if you are now with a partner, be aware of the fact that you are likely to be alone and financially responsible for yourself at some point in your life.
- Recognize that too many other-oriented women who don't take charge of their own financial destiny end up as a terrible financial burden to their children.
- Be sure your parents are taken care of so you won't be supporting them later on.
- Model a healthy financial person for your children.

EXERCISES

1. List the times this week you put yourself second. Stop at ten.

2. List three times this week that someone put you first. Hard to do?

3. List three times this week you were definitely self-caring, making your own security and well-being a priority. How about two times? One? Well, come back to this next week.

4. Decide how you will plan your long-term financial goals. Will you visit a financial planner? Read two books? Attend a class or seminar? Give yourself a deadline.

5. Calculate how much money you could have in a mutual fund in five years if you passed up the $2.50 coffee and muffin four days a week, 50 weeks a year. Yup, $2,500. If you pass it up five days a week, you'd have more than $3,000! And that's without any growth or interest. Now calculate what you'd have if you socked away 10 percent of your total income.

6. Do you do your own taxes? If not, why not? Do you understand your tax return? If not, why not?

7. Are your parents financially secure? If not, what can you do to help them today for the future?

Building Wealth without a Business

Perhaps you have absolutely no interest in operating your own company. While there can be big rewards in running your own business, there are plenty of pitfalls, risks, and responsibilities, with long hours, hard work, and sometimes overwhelming pressures. It is certainly not right for everyone.

Is it possible to become a millionairess without the hassle of going into business for yourself? You bet. Here are some other ways.

STRIKE IT RICH IN SOMEONE ELSE'S BUSINESS

It's been said that you can't get rich working for someone else. Well, like all things, that too has changed, especially in

California's Silicon Valley where *Business Week* reports some-times even the receptionists are millionaires.

In 1993, for example, Heather Beach walked into a shabby brick building in East Palo Alto, California, to take a reception-ist job for Siebel Systems, Inc., a start-up company producing sales information software. The octopus-type position and a $7,000 pay cut didn't bother Heather. She was pursuing her goal of working at an exciting new company where she had a chance of becoming a millionaire by age 30.

How did she do it? Like many of her colleagues, she elected to take a chunk of her paycheck in equity on top of stock op-tions she already received. Siebel went public in June, 1996 at $17 a share. By December, it had more than quadrupled in value and Beach's fortunes soared, too. For every dollar she ac-cepted in stock options instead of cash, she earned at least $40, depending on the stock price.

Personnel assistant Jennifer Overstreet, 36, worked for Oracle Corporation for 12 years, starting at an annual salary of $18,000. In that time Oracle grew from 35 employees to 24,000 and from $5 million in revenues to $5 billion. Her bank account swelled too, as stock options originally granted for $5 each became worth at least $2,000, thanks to some 36 stock splits.

Because money attracts money, moving to a center of wealth can be a way to wealth without going into business. It all adds up: better wages, benefits, stock options, bonuses, and oppor-tunities for advancement. Something to consider.

BECOMING A MASTER MONEY MANAGER

On the other hand, maybe you don't want to work outside the home—not for yourself and not for someone else. Perhaps you have young children or a disability that keeps you home.

There is still a way to attain your financial goals, whether short or long term. It's slow, but it's steady. You must simply become a master money manager.

Let's say you're a typical stay-at-home mom. Your role is housewife and mother while hubby brings home a steady paycheck. You have no outside income of your own, but you still want to *earn* something for the family. Does this scenario ring a bell?

Remember, you already have plenty of skills that you've developed in your role as CEO of your home. Running a home, after all, is similar to running a corporation. There are schedules to be followed, duties to be performed, deliveries to be completed, order to be maintained, deadlines to be met, and safety measures to be attained.

Do you realize how fully qualified and disciplined you are? Over a period of time, and with the best boot camp training (provided by your family), you've perfected patience and endurance. These are two absolute necessities for a successful financial leader.

You don't have to be a college graduate to be financially successful, although it is to your advantage if you are. A degree can speed up the race to financial freedom. But any goal can be reached. It is up to you to make it happen. Best of all, it can begin in the privacy and comfort of your home—your safety zone. Let's agree that your new venture is to improve your family's financial status.

Perhaps in the past you've made some bad financial decisions. You can't change the past, but you can design your future as if it were a business. In fact, the perfect first step is to write a business plan for your family's future. (See Lesson 13.) Putting the figures down in black and white will make it real.

Your executive summary should include your goal in specific dollar terms—whether it is becoming completely free of debt (except, perhaps, a mortgage) in 18 months, having the cash for a down payment on a new home in two years, or a longer-term goal such as a college fund for your children or developing a substantial investment portfolio to provide you with a comfortable retirement.

If you have a partner, sit down together to review your business plan for the future. Decide how much you must save each week to reach your goal. Then see where you can *earn* those dollars.

THE TRAP OF SMALL INDULGENCES

People who grew up during the Depression scrimped for every extra dime. They carried a bag lunch to work—if they had a job. They made a fryer last a week for a family of four, slivering the meat from the scrawny neck bone for the Saturday night soup. They let down their daughters' dresses as they grew, and covered up the old hem line with a bit of ribbon.

In the '30s, they invested ten cents a week in savings bonds. In the '40s, they invested in stocks or company investment plans. In the '50s and '60s, their kids scoffed at them for being way too careful with their money. Surprise. Today, a lot of those Depression survivors are quiet millionaires. Their golden years really are golden as they enjoy their retirements and their grandkids and create substantial family trusts.

On the other hand, too many people today seem to feel that accumulating large sums is impossible. They feel vaguely entitled to all the things their parents have without going the way their parents did. Because these people don't have the cash for a new car, they buy it on time and end up paying considerably more than the sticker price with the interest. Because they don't have the down payment for even a small home, they rent a ritzy apartment and add it to their monthly credit card payments. Then, because they don't have any money left to invest, they shrug and treat themselves to a *small indulgence* instead. "Hey, I'm working hard," they say. "I deserve this."

Well, perhaps they do deserve it, but do the math. Say they have a cappuccino every day on the way to work. Or they get a fancy sandwich at a deli down the street for lunch. Or they go to the latest movie instead of renting a video of something they missed last year. Remember our lesson on not squandering money? Put it to work in *every* part of your life!

TIME IS MONEY

Small sums, you say. But they add up. Boy, do they add up! Time is money, you say. That's absolutely true. And by spending some time, you could save some money.

Let's rewrite that small indulgences script.

Have our constant small spenders buy a small Thermos and brew cappuccino at home just four days a week at a saving of $2 a day. Make a sandwich instead of buying it four days a week and save $3. Enjoying a video at home with their partner instead of standing in line on a Saturday night saves at least $11.

At the end of a year, just with those small adjustments, they'd have accumulated more than $1,600!

Here's our challenge. Become a master money manager for one month. Challenge yourself to be a tightwad—just for 30 days. Don't leave the *saved* money in your wallet where it can disappear. Actually put the cash you save into a bank or jar or shoebox that you label My Future Fortune.

Here are eight ideas to get you started:

1. *Always pay yourself first.* Take $100 from every paycheck and put it in your millionairess bank before spending another cent.

2. *Grocery shopping.* You've read these ideas over and over in newspapers and magazines. Now, just for 30 days, do it! Plan your menu and make a list before shopping. Eat vegetarian at least once a week. Don't shop when you're hungry. Try store brands. Use coupons and rebates. Check sales. Keep your eyes down—lower-profit items (better value for us!) are on shelves below eye level. Carry a notepad and jot down your savings (difference between regular and sale price). Plunk the savings (and all your loose change) in your millionairess bank when you get home. If you've been a careless shopper until now, you could be saving anywhere from $20 to $100 or more a month.

3. *Buying clothes.* Never buy clothing that requires dry cleaning. You have to pay over and over again. Locate upscale consignment shops where you can get gently used, quality clothing for a fraction of the original price. Buy one top-quality classic outfit instead of three trendy, poorly made garments. Have a same-sized friend? Consider swapping seldom-worn dressy outfits and halve your costs. Comparison shop. Bring only as much cash as you want to spend. When it's gone, so are you. Possible savings: up to $100 per outfit.

4. *Telephone.* Write a letter (or even better, use e-mail). Comparison shop among long-distance carriers—they are extremely competitive these days. A neighbor recently got an $80 check in the mail. Endorsing it meant she'd automatically switch carriers. Instead she called her own carrier and learned if she mailed the check to them, they would credit the amount to her account. Lesson: If you see a particularly good offer, call your own carrier. They will often match someone trying to lure you away. You can probably save $10 or more per month depending on your phone usage. Feed your bank again.

5. *Energy bills.* Turn off lights when rooms are not in use; use microwave instead of oven; fill up dishwasher; repair dripping faucets or leaking toilets; conserve heat or air-conditioning by closing off unused rooms; don't overuse hot water; lower thermostat; install ceiling fans; replace incandescent bulbs with fluorescent; invest in a whole-house fan for summer. Possible savings: at least $20 per month. Fatten your bank some more!

6. *Entertainment.* Visit your library. Many these days have magazines, videos, and books on tape to borrow along with books for adults and children. Wait for new movies to come out on video and pop your own popcorn. Possible savings: approximately $40 each time a family of four rents a video instead of going to the movies.

7. *Life rituals.* Be careful! Holidays and life rituals can upset your goal. Lower holiday spending and gift giving by shopping throughout the year during sales. Preholiday retail prices always zoom upward. Remember, it isn't the most expensive gift that says the most. For example, instead of a $100 watch, one mother gave her son a framed 60-million-year-old fish fossil ($17 at a craft show) for high school graduation. She also wrote a letter about how she hoped the ancient fish would help him keep things in perspective when the going got tough. (He's now the 35-year-old CFO of an international major money management company with the framed fossil on his wall.) Possible savings: could be very substantial over a year's time.

8. *Love those white elephants.* We must confess, we women are the consumers of the world. We buy and buy. We like new things, new fashions, new furniture, new houses, and new cars. That's all well and good. It's what you do with these things after you are through with them that brings in cash-ola. You guessed it—sell them. Find a consignment

store for things still in good condition. Have a garage sale, boutique sale, neighborhood sale, at-work sale, association sale. With all the stuff we collect there probably isn't a woman alive who couldn't rake in a quick $500 if she really tried. Fine, go ahead and chuckle. But let's look at a big picture. The 1996 *Guiness Book of Records* says: The Cleveland Convention Center White Elephant sale held October 18-19, 1983, raised $427,935.21! The greatest amount of money raised at a one-day sale was $214,085.99 organized by the Winnetka Congregational Church, Winnetka, Illinois, on May 12, 1994. Bet they laughed all the way to the bank. Consider a neighborhood garage sale—sharing the cost of advertising, but keeping your own earnings. There are books about how to hold a successful sale. Maybe you can find the book at someone else's sale and buy it secondhand!

A lot of these ideas require a whole new frame of mind—one focused on the long term rather than get-what-I-want-when-I-want-it. The people who never save are the people who will be struggling to make ends meet when they're in their 60s.

The people who are prudent and careful today may well be cruising the Caribbean in their 50s, happily retired on their steady investment income.

EXERCISES

1. Start saving today. Make saving a regular expense, not an elective. Stop buying things you don't need. Don't reward yourself with things.

2. Set money savings and spending goals: daily, weekly, monthly, annually, 5 year, 10 year, 15 year, and so on. (Concentrate on the daily.)

3. Write a business plan for your family.

4. Eliminate debt. Eat beans, rice, and salad until you pay off credit card obligations. If you have a car loan, pay it off, then keep the car until you can pay cash for the next one.

Why Pay Interest? Earn It!

If you paid attention in the last lesson, you should have been able to save at least $100 in one month's time, simply by keeping track of how much you thought you had to spend and how much you actually did spend, saving the difference. You're getting the message—it really is easy to grow your money!

Another great reward resulting from these applied strategies is that they work for anyone, regardless of age or income. You can build up a pretty tidy sum if you start now and invest diligently for the next 20 years or so.

You can save even if you live on a shoestring. Remember the turtle that beat the hare in the race? You will get there, too. As you develop the habit of putting money in your millionairess bank, you become encouraged by the rising balance. Moreover, you will automatically discover more cutbacks by taking charge of your cash.

You have arrived at the great moment that will reward your efforts of conservation. You are now ready to start investing.

START INVESTING TODAY

Albert Einstein was once asked to name the greatest discovery of the 20th century. Most expected him to refer to his theory of relativity, nuclear energy, or some other important scientific development. His answer: "Compound interest."

Compound interest works like this: If you invest $100 per month for 20 years (a total investment of $24,000), you will have earned an interest of $17,103 at 5 percent; $51,937 at 10 percent. Add that to your original savings and you have quite a nice sum of money. Imagine how much you'd have if you invested even larger sums?

Even if you only have a small amount of money to invest, start now. The sooner you start, the sooner your money will grow. Sometimes small investors believe that their options are limited. Not so. There are many investment vehicles to take advantage of. Banks, brokerage firms, insurance companies, and financial planners are competing for your cash whether you have $100 or $5,000. Major financial institutions always have a new gimmick to entice the novice investor. So be wary.

Read a lot, talk to successful investors you know, and shop around, even with only $100 to spare. Eventually, you will become a larger investor. Become informed by reading and learning about the maze of money vehicles and the art of making smart decisions.

Learn how to analyze your options as you watch your money grow from $100 to $5,000 and so on. Make a point of setting aside some time to learn about handling your money and exploring the finance world. Consider taking a course in financial planning. Then take as many courses as you can in investing! It's worth the time and effort because it is *your money*.

A pleasant thought: There is nothing more satisfying than the contented feeling of knowing that your bills are paid and you have money in the bank.

Need more encouragement? Well, take Molly Bukaty, 23, of Overland Park, Kansas, who, on a dollar a day, launched her saving plan two years ago and already has $1,500 in the bank. According to *Woman's Day,* she began by putting $30 a month, plus extras such as tax refunds and birthday money, into a savings account.

After hitting $2,000, Molly plans to keep half in the bank and invest the rest in a mutual fund. Her goal: $5,000 for a down payment on a house and $1,000 to start her retirement egg. "When I retire," she says, "I want to do it comfortably."

Molly is off to a terrific start—and just imagine how your money will build by investing small sums over a period of 20 or 30 years!

INVESTMENT CLUBS

Another adventure is the Beardstown Ladies' approach of pooling your money with other women to make stock market investments. This group of women formed an investment club and wrote books about how others could form investment clubs. Their books sold well (despite some recent controversy) and investment clubs began sprouting up all over the country.

The Beardstown Ladies and most other investment clubs are affiliated with a large national association called the National Association of Investors Corporation, or the NAIC. These folks have lots of information available on how to form a club and how to operate a club. Dedicated to educating ordinary folks across the country about the power of investing, the NAIC also sponsors many educational seminars and investors fairs. To contact them, call 248-583-6242 or visit their Web site at www. better-investing.org.

Another example of a successful club is the Mahogany Association, an investment club of 12 African-American women.

They began with $50 per month, when six sisters from Delta Sigma Theta sorority decided they wanted some extra cash for a national convention in San Francisco. Startled by their accumulation, they continued investing $50 per month and a club member visited a Merrill Lynch office in Canton, Ohio. In 1996, the group's net worth was more than $100,000, including $70,000 in stocks and another $30,000 in cash.

There are many investment clubs around the country. You can find a club that needs new members, or you can form your own with friends. Most clubs start off with fairly small monthly contributions, $25 or $50 a month from each member, but as the club and its members age sometimes the members agree to raise the contributions. And it all combines to grow bigger and bigger and bigger.

INVESTMENT PRIORITIES

Your very first investment goal must be accumulating a safety net of funds in an absolutely safe place such as a bank account or a mutual fund money market. But keep in mind that the money you park in the bank is never going to grow in the same proportion that money invested other ways will. Only keep three to six months expenses in the bank, and invest the rest in something with a higher return.

Once you are ready to start investing for growth, one practical initial investment method is dollar cost averaging in an index fund with a respected no-load mutual fund such as Fidelity, Vanguard, or T. Rowe Price. There are dozens of other excellent funds as well.

Dollar cost averaging means you invest a certain amount on a regular basis. These same dollars buy fewer shares when the price is high and more shares when the price is low. But you just keep putting the money in, month after month, watching the shares and the value grow. Occasionally, investors will stumble on a real high-flying stock, but when you are investing for the long term, adopt the slow-and-steady habits of the tortoise.

Index funds are simply mutual funds that mimic the stock market as a whole. They usually have lower management costs than other funds.

A *no-load fund* is one that does not charge you a fee directly or through commission.

Remember, investing in the stock market is a long-term proposition. Many investors shudder when recalling the October crash of 1987 or the disastrous drops in the late summer of 1998.

Call at least two mutual funds and ask for new investor literature. Discover the difference between a load fund and a no-load fund. Study the various kinds of funds: bond funds, money market funds, equity funds, index balanced funds.

Usually the mutual fund literature will identify the goals of individual funds—growth, tax-advantaged, or income—and spell out suggested *mixes* of funds for various life stages. By law, all prospectuses must use similar formats to show the value of their funds so you easily can compare them.

If you haven't done any investing before, it can be a scary move. But your money won't multiply under your mattress. The long-term average for the U.S. stock markets and the mutual funds that invest in them is around 9 percent per year. Get advice from someone who is doing well financially. Don't fall for get-rich-quick plans that involve dessert at a local hotel before you hear the pitch.

Another potential golden egg is the new Roth IRA. While the contributions are not tax-deductible, the money accumulates tax-free and there is no tax to pay when you withdraw it upon retirement. The younger you are, the more fantastic this opportunity is. Be sure to educate yourself on this wealth builder before Congress notices what a good deal it is for individuals!

EXERCISES

1. Engrave this in your mind: Interest is something you *earn,* not something you *pay.*

2. Within your own family, circle of friends, or neighborhood, find a good money manager who can help you get started.

3. Instead of letting your savings sit in your local bank, learn about mutual funds. Check the *Morningstar Report* at your local library or on the Internet. Review the annual mutual fund rating issues of *Money* or *Kiplinger's.*

4. Start a Roth IRA with a mutual fund family.

5. Start watching financial programs on TV. Listen to radio talk shows about money.

Develop Multiple Income Streams: Copyright, Patent, Trademark

Future income is money you will receive next month, next year, or even year after year after year through today's efforts. It's using today's work to create future earnings. In fact, you could say it's like harvesting two or three or ten crops with just one planting.

The main idea behind building future income is to make your money work hard for you. Because there are only so many hours in the day for earning, you want to simultaneously develop other streams of income.

Royalties from books or inventions are one example of future income. Buying a *fixer-upper,* repairing it, then renting it, might be a way to provide another income stream. Franchising your great idea is another potential source of future payments. Selling your company (and starting another one) is yet another because such deals often include some sort of payment over time.

COPYRIGHTS

Here's an example of how a book copyright created future income and put author Gloria Naylor, 48, on the road to being a millionairess. Gloria Naylor belongs to the late 20th-century phenomenon of black women who have made fortunes on what is known as *intellectual property.*

She, along with such authors as Toni Morrison, Alice Walker, Terry McMillan, Maya Angelou, and Jamaica Kincaid, have neared or topped the million-dollar mark writing books that reflect the rich, complex lives of black women.

Naylor completed Yale's graduate program in Afro-American studies in 1983, the same year her first book *The Women of Brewster Place* was published. It was an instant triumph, winning the American Book Award for best first fiction. Four years later Oprah Winfrey paid her $50,000 for television rights and produced *The Women of Brewster Place* as a two-part miniseries in which she, Oprah, starred. Since then Naylor has published four more novels: *Mama Day, Linden Hills, Bailey's Cafe,* and last year's *The Men of Brewster Place.*

Her literary success has greatly increased the offers from publishers. For example, she received a $5,000 advance for *The Women of Brewster Place* in 1983. In 1996, her fourth novel, *The Men of Brewster Place,* received an advance of $900,000!

Authors are paid royalties on each book sold—typically a percentage of the sales price. The advance is a portion of those royalties paid before the book is published. Once the advance is earned back (that is, royalties equal to the advance have been earned), the royalties are paid to the writer on a semiannual or annual basis.

Naylor has been prudent with her earnings. "When I started to make money from writing," Naylor says, "I lived as if I didn't have it. You have to live a little bit under your means to accumulate money. *The Women of Brewester Place* came out when I was still in graduate school. I didn't touch that $5,000 advance. I did the same with *Linden Hills,* which got a $25,000 advance."

The result of her hard work and prudent financial management has been financial security and the prospect of a wealthy retirement. Naylor has incorporated and formed a company, One Way Productions, to generate educational and entertainment material for young people. She's also working to produce *Mama Day* as a film.

She earns between $5,000 and $7,000 for a speaking engagement and continues to receive royalties for each of her books, including *The Women of Brewster Place,* which was first published more than ten years ago, but continues to be popular.

Her investments include a brownstone in Brooklyn bought for $425,000 and assessed for $750,000, as well as a Sea Island home purchased for $115,000 and now valued at $200,000.

Her other retirement investments include mutual funds and a Keogh Plan—a financial vehicle for self-employed people. She plans to keep writing and to pay off all her mortgages by the time she is 60. "I never like dealing with money," she confesses, "but the older I get, the more I realize I have to. My writing is a business that I run from my desk."

Remember, although a publisher publishes your book, unless it was a work-for-hire project, the copyright is yours. You end up licensing various rights to the publishing house. These rights can include things like foreign sales, movie or television rights, serialization, and merchandising, and are negotiated and spelled-out in a contract. Always use an agent or literary attorney when negotiating such a contract.

Legally, everything you write is copyrighted when you write it. However, you must register that copyright to protect yourself if litigation arises. Registration costs only $20. You can get a copyright on things you publish yourself or sell to another to be published. These can include among other things: books, poetry, plays, songs, catalogues, photographs, computer programs, advertisements, labels, movies, maps, drawings, sculpture, prints and art reproductions, game boards, and rules or instructions.

You also can get a copyright on a graphic design, a T-shirt design, or a product's appearance. To learn what may and may not be copyrighted, simply write to the Copyright Office, Washington, DC 20559.

You may think you can't write a book or a song or a game, but there are literally thousands published each year. If you have a passion for something, consider sharing it with other people—for money.

Today, many people are acting as their own publishers. Distribution and marketing are major commitments for people who self-publish (as "independents"), but the rewards can be substantial. For example, take a book that costs $2.50 to produce when you factor in editorial costs, illustrations, cover art, and printing. If you price it at $17.95, you'll make more than $15 per book, while a royalty might be only $1.79 or less. Your cost will be less on subsequent printings, so if you write an *evergreen* book that sells over a long time, you'll have created future income.

Bettina, for example, has an evergreen book providing her with additional income.

> *Bettina: I originally self-published* Chiquita's Cocoon, *selling some 20,000 copies. When publishers came calling, I got an agent and the book was auctioned off, landing me a six-figure contract. Throughout both publishing experiences, I earned additional income by lecturing and leading seminars, and through back room sales. Another stream of income grew from the book sales to schools, colleges, and universities that made* Chiquita *required reading—thereby giving me sizable classroom orders. It is still selling strong today!*

Another independent publisher who makes money through the Internet is the reknown "kidney stone lady," Gail Golomb from Roseville, California. She says of her second edition of *The Kidney Stones Handbook: A Patient's Guide to Hope, Cure and Prevention* (Four Geez Press, $17.95), "Of a 10,000 printing, I believe 5,000 were sold (at full retail price) to actual Web visitors." Gail is listed with ReadersNdex.com (as opposed to Amazon.com) because "I felt I got more Web space." *The Kidney Stones Handbook* has been one of ReadersNdex's top heavy hitters. You can browse it in depth at www.readersndex.com/fourgeez. Gail's book is an evergreen classic because it's written for and from the patient's viewpoint. In 1997 she launched *The Kidney Stones Network Newsletter* and has plans in the works for The International Kidney Stones Foundation. Beyond that is even more branching off, perhaps, a cookbook, diet book, and selling related medical books. Indeed, the kidney stone lady just keeps rolling along.

Oh, and one book that we all know very well and was originally self-published is *The Wizard of Oz!* Talk about future income.

PATENTS

Patents are a whole 'nother ballgame—complicated, expensive, and often unnecessary. You don't need a patent to introduce a product. In fact, many products on the market don't have patents. So don't spend the money unless the patent can pay for itself. On the other hand, if you're looking for capital to develop your product, or you plan to license it, then holding a patent pending may impress investors and licensers and may protect your idea.

Unfortunately, it's a fallacy to believe that a patent totally protects an invention. In reality, if anyone infringes on your patent, it's up to you to take action through a time-consuming, expensive lawsuit. Remember too, we live in a superfast global world. Something patented in the United States today can be *knocked off* tomorrow in China.

Nevertheless, patents have made many folks wealthy. Two people who really cleaned up with profitable patents are Joy Mangano, creator of the Miracle Mop, with a total of $80 million in sales, and Jon Nokes, creator of the SmartMop, with $44 million in annual sales. That's a lot of mopping up.

Back in 1989, Mangano, a mother of three, found herself at the mercy of sponges, paper towels, and mops that didn't last very long. Her solution: a sturdy plastic mop with a unique self-wringing action. QVC, a cable shopping channel, took on her product but initial sales petered out quickly. Then Mangano took over, giving her own live, on-screen pitch right from her heart—and sold 18,000 mops in 20 minutes! It seems she's been on QVC ever since. Mangano holds that patent as well as others.

The $44-million mop guy went the way of direct-response TV. Nokes paid Concepts Video Productions in Montville, New Jersey, $60,000 for a 28-minute infomercial. Orders poured in. After the initial television buying frenzy, Nokes still went on to greener pastures, selling to Wal-Mart and Kmart, whose sales surpassed direct TV sales.

If you live in a sizable city, see if your library offers a patent depository library on computer. What people invent and hold as a patent or patent pending will blow your mind! Also, if you're the curious type, pick up almost any product in a store, look for the patent pending symbol, write down the number, and look up the details in the library.

TRADEMARKS

In its most literal meaning, a trademark is any word or other symbol that is consistently attached to goods to identify and distinguish them from others in the marketplace. Companies defend their trademarks vigorously because if they are used too often in public, they lose their rights to them.

The words *Procter & Gamble* are a tradename, while *Kleenex*™ is a trademark. The term *trademark* is also commonly used to mean service marks as in *NBC,* certification marks as in the *Good Housekeeping seal of approval,* and collective marks as in *FDIC.*

Trademark law deals with the degree to which the owner of a name used in marketing goods or services will be afforded a monopoly over the use of the name. An example in Sacramento, California, was a very small coffee shop called the Red Robin. An out-of-state restaurant chain called the Red Robin wanted to open several eateries in Sacramento, but was prevented from using the name unless the existing Red Robin gave—or more likely, sold—the right to it.

To register a trademark in your state, call or write your Secretary of State office. To register federally, write to the Patent and Trademark Office, Washington, DC 20231.

EXERCISES

1. Do you have a book in you? What are people always asking you about? What is your area of flair? Your knowledge or expertise?

2. If you have a product to sell, watch infomercials on television. Consult television production companies to learn the costs.

3. Another route for selling products is through the cable shopping channels. If you have an item, contact them to find out how you might provide your product or even appear with it. These folks are easy to reach and easy to talk with.

4. Have someone else distribute and market your wares. Scout out catalogs related to your product and contact the company.

5. Expand your horizons and diversify.

Read and Grow Rich—Be an Information Sponge

Read and grow rich? Oh, it sounds much too easy. To lie on the couch all afternoon reading an enjoyable book and grow rich as a result—wouldn't that be wonderful if it were true? Well, we believe that it is! We believe that by reading a wealth of material your life will grow rich as a result. How rich will you be? You'll be:

- Rich with the confidence that others have triumphed and prospered and you will too!
- Rich with information and knowledge about how others succeeded.
- Rich with admiration for the hard work and struggles of others and the amount of time and effort required.
- Rich with the possibility of all that life can offer should you just go out and boldly seek it!

Too often we feel trapped by our lives, trapped by the way our lives are at that exact moment and unable to move forward or make positive changes. In Lesson 8 you learned techniques to help you focus on the future instead of the past. Here you will begin to learn from the pasts of others in order to enrich your own future!

CAN YOU REALLY READ AND GROW RICH?

How exactly can reading make you rich? The answer is simple, yet powerful. Reading can make you rich by teaching you how others have done it. If we feel stuck in our lives, focused on what is happening around us, for a few quiet hours we can step outside of our own existence and enter that of someone else. Just pick up a book to expand your thinking.

Do you harbor dreams of building a big money-making business on a national scale someday? There are plenty of books out there that will help you see how others have done it. But not the dry, step-by-step business books that fill the shelves. Reach instead for the stories that are filled with the dramatic ups and downs of establishing a business. Reach for the stories that will invite you to share the daily struggles of the founder as she, too, attempts to leave behind past failures (and you will soon learn how common past failure is among the supersuccessful!) and build a prosperous future.

Read and grow rich with the information shared by Howard Schulz in his book *Pour Your Heart Into It,* in which he tells the story of how he built the Starbucks coffee empire. Was he successful from day one? Far from it! He couldn't even get hired by the original guys who started Starbucks. But he persisted; he went back and pleaded his case. And once he was hired, he steadily worked his way into a position where he could one day buy the company and launch it on a much larger scale.

Overnight success? No. A slow and steady success he can sit back and savor now over a cup of his rich, black coffee? Mmmmm, delicious!

Spend a Saturday morning in the library or bookstore. Who else is sharing their personal story of hard-won success? The late Sam Walton of Wal-Mart shared his struggles in a book called *Made in America*. He didn't build the enormous Wal-Mart chain in a day. He worked day after day, year after year to pursue his dream, exactly the same way that you will have to.

And can you learn anything from Wayne Huizenga? On the few corners where Howard Schulz doesn't have a Starbucks, you'll find a Blockbuster. Learn how that company was built in *The Making of Blockbuster: How Wayne Huizenga Built a Sports and Entertainment Empire from Trash, Grit, and Videotape*. He built his business from trash? What does that mean? It means that Wayne's first business was the garbage business—not exactly one filled with glamour and prestige. Imagine what his family and friends must have said to him when he revealed his dreams for greater things: "Wayne, give it up! You're in the garbage business, pal." But he didn't give up.

Hey, what's with all these examples of men in a book about millionairesses? Remember, if you want to succeed, you have to hang out with successful people. You have to read all you can about successful people and how they got they way. By reading about them, you can hang out with them in the privacy of your own home! So build the biggest group possible, don't just restrict yourself to only reading about successful women.

ELIMINATE ENVY

One of the traps that we can all easily fall prey to on the road to success is envy. Envy for the fancy things that supersuccessful people have, the big houses that they live in, the exotic places that they go. All of their *stuff*. But by reading the full story behind their rise (or resurrection) we can move beyond the envy we feel for their things and learn the how and the why of their extraordinary journey.

Katherine Graham inspires envy in many of us. A wealthy and powerful woman, surely she must have had an easy time of it? What is there to learn from the story of a little rich girl who ended up running her daddy's newspaper? Plenty. Her book, *Personal History*, reveals in painful detail what it was like to grow up as the child of a big businessman and a well-known and talented mother. To marry a man you adored, only to learn he was deeply flawed. And the shock of her husband's suicide, which ultimately thrust her into control of the *Washington Post*. She did learn to run the paper. The media company she headed did grow in astonishing ways. But was it easy? No. Should we envy her? No. Should we learn from her? Yes.

Television personality Star Jones has much to teach us in her book *You Have to Stand for Something or You'll Fall for Anything*. Sure, her life is pretty fabulous now. But her book traces her entire path from a small town in North Carolina to her current seat next to Barbara Walters on the ABC show *The View*. Envy her? No. Learn from her? Please do.

What can we learn from the lives of bold and adventurous women? When feeling trapped in our everyday lives, unable to see our next positive move, are there books that will help us capture the feel of wind in our faces and let our spirits soar? Read about the life of Beryl Markham, pioneer aviatrix in Africa. Her book *West with the Night* is filled with such inspiring and adventurous prose that Ernest Hemingway said, "She can write rings around all of us who consider ourselves writers." Let her description of her dashing life inspire you to do something dashing the very next day!

Emily Hahn, the late magazine and book writer, lived an extraordinary life of daring and adventure. Her biography *Nobody Said Not to Go* will open your eyes to the possibilities that she saw when all the women around her lived lives of convention and constraint. And she continued that life of daring well into her 90s, walking every day to her office at *The New Yorker.*

Amelia Earhart, the famed pilot, played a big part in her own packaging and publicity, the very things that brought her to worldwide prominence over many other (and better) women pilots. Reading biographies about Amelia Erhart will help enrich your sense of how effective publicity can build a reputation overnight.

Other adventurous women like Gertrude Bell *(Desert Queen)* and Isabella Bird *(Amazing Traveler: Isabella Bird)* will help you see that throughout history women have been bold and daring enough to venture to places they were not encouraged to go. Gertrude Bell spent most of her adult life in the Middle East (over her proper British family's strong objections) and Isabella Bird explored the West, Hawaii, and Japan on her own in the 19th century. If they could do that, what is holding you back from attempting equally daring things in this day and age? In the spirit of Gertrude and Isabella, get out there and pursue your dream!

Shifting our focus back to the 20th century, who among us knows that in the 1920s much of the screenwriting business was controlled by women? Think how much richer your knowledge will be after reading *Without Lying Down: Frances Marion and the Powerful Women of Early Hollywood.* Do you dream of a fulfilling and well-paid career in the entertainment business? Then you'd better sit down and read and grow rich from the life of Frances Marion.

Any other women making big money in the entertainment business? For the past few summers the rock concert scene has been dominated by the Lilith Fair, an all women's concert—a bold idea. Who had the nerve to organize that? Learn all about it in *Building a Mystery: The Story of Sarah McLachlan & Lilith Fair.* Read and grow rich with admiration for how hard she worked to get it off the ground.

In the glamorous worlds of fashion, magazines, and the movies lie three more stories to help remind you that women can create extraordinary opportunities for themselves: Coco Chanel, Clare Booth Luce, and Dawn Steel. Coco Chanel, who started life in humble circumstances, built an international business. So why can't you? There are inspiring books published on Chanel every few years, as she continues to be an object of admiration. Clare Booth Luce was not hired as an editor, but showed up for work and sat at a desk anyway. After a few weeks, she was quietly added to the payroll. From her first small start in the '20s at *Vanity Fair* she went on to a career as a journalist, playwright, and ultimately, ambassador to Italy. You'll find *Rage for Fame: The Ascent of Clare Booth Luce* on your library shelves from which you can glean the lessons that Clare can teach. The late Dawn Steel got her first taste of the entrepreneurial life selling designer toilet paper (wild, but true) before entering the movie business and ultimately becoming one of the few women to head a major movie studio. Her autobiography is called *They Can Kill You but They Can't Eat You: Lessons from the Front.* You, too, will find rich inspiration, information, and possibilities in her tale.

FICTIONAL HEROINES TO GUIDE YOU

Can we also read and grow rich from novels? Many a well-crafted tale of a young woman who beats the odds and prospers on her own can bring richness to our thoughts and dreams.

Bettina: I read Gone with the Wind *when I was 14, and I have drawn inspiration from the example of Scarlett ever since. She was bold, she was tough, she wasn't afraid of hard work, and she loved money and success. If I hadn't found the story of*

Scarlett O'Hara when I did, I think that my life would have turned out much different.

Novels can open our eyes to many possibilities in life and give you the sense that there are many other ways to live. The next time you pick up a novel, ask yourself as you are reading: "What can I learn from this? Does this inspire me to try new things?" Look for novels that draw you into other worlds, other ways of living and doing, and you will bring additional richness to your life.

And how can we overlook the tremendous power of inspirational books? The true purpose of books like *The Millionairess Across the Street, Think and Grow Rich, The Richest Man in Babylon,* and other motivational money books is to keep you excited about the *possibilities* in life. When your blood starts pumping and your mind starts spinning over something you read in a motivational book, get out there and *do it!*

For many years Bettina bought copies of Catherine Ponder's *The Dynamic Laws of Prosperity* to pass out to family and friends. Jennifer has bought and given away multiple copies of *Do What You Love and the Money Will Follow.* Motivational books really do inspire millions of people every year to reach beyond their boundaries—join them.

Remember, the more you read, the richer you and your life will become!

EXERCISES

1. Hop in your car now and head for the library! Check out a big stack of books that catch your eye and get to work learning from the lives of others.

2. Imagine the title of your autobiography years from now. Write it down and add it to your list of goals.

3. Start a *Read and Grow Rich* journal in which you write down what you have learned from the books, lives, and advice of others. Write down quotes, inspirational phrases and ideas, as well as mistakes that you will try to avoid making yourself!

LESSON 21

Philanthropists All—
Be Generous with
Your Time and Money

Lesson after lesson throughout this small book we have encouraged you to go out and accumulate wealth. It is your duty to prosper and thrive—both personally and financially. But it is also your duty to be caring and thoughtful towards fellow human beings. The best way to fulfill those obligations as a human is to be philanthropic.

Philanthropic? What a fancy and mysterious word! Jennifer remembers hearing it first as a young girl watching the *Batman* television show. Bruce Wayne (who was secretly Batman) was always described as a *millionaire philanthropist*. Sounds like a great thing to be, Jennifer thought, and so when other little girls in the '60s wanted to be nurses or teachers, she wanted to be a millionaire philanthropist!

Philanthropy is defined as "love of mankind, benevolence, concerned with human welfare and the reduction of suffering." What beautiful ideas.

Philanthropic acts not only benefit those on whose behalf you are working, or donating money, but you will benefit as well. All good deeds will be returned to you, most often in unexpected ways. The universe will reward you. Send a check to a charity, and later that day receive a phone call about a large contract! Spend an afternoon helping at a retirement home focusing on the lives of others, and soon someone important will focus their attention on you. There are countless stories about real riches that have arrived unexpectedly just after someone either made a charity pledge or donation, or gave of themselves and their time. Selfless giving sparks unlimited receiving!

One of the most basic of philanthropic principles is tithing. Most of us have heard of tithing before, it is a habit much encouraged by many churches as it has biblical roots. In Hebrew, the word *tithe* means *tenth*. So tithing involves giving one-tenth of all of your income to church or charity. And unlike the tithing that we seem to do to the U.S. government in the form of taxes, this kind of tithing has long been believed to benefit the giver as well as the receiver. Tithe, and your money and goodwill, will be returned to you tenfold, a hundredfold, or even a thousandfold! All good deeds, all charitable acts and donations, will ultimately contribute back to you. You will be a richer person as a result. Richer because of the pleasure and help that you have given to others, richer because of the pleasure you feel in giving money or time, and richer financially because all good deeds multiply.

Do you want to give to others, but feel that 10 percent is too much for you to handle right now? Give 10 percent of your time. To give lovingly and selflessly of your time is equally as valuable as writing out a check, and will result in as much reward coming back to you. Follow the extraordinary example of Jimmy and Rosalyn Carter, who after leaving the Oval Office have devoted years of service to working with Habitat for Humanity, building houses for the less fortunate. Contact the local office in your community, chances are they are going out to build yet another house this very weekend!

Throughout this book we also have encouraged you to become a more active investor in order to accumulate wealth. Giving is another form of investing. In the same way that you put your money into a favorite stock, buy a prime piece of real estate, or buy into a mutual find, choosing a charity to help is just as much of an investment.

But all investments should have a return. Where does the return come on your charitable investments? The returns come from within. And these returns come back to you much more quickly than longer range financial investments! Instantaneous, in fact. The warm feeling of helping your fellow man, the chance to see a smile on an otherwise grim and defeated face, the tremendous charge that comes from being a part of an active group. These returns are extraordinarily high!

It is the responsibility of great wealth to be greatly philanthropic. Both Bill Gates and Warren Buffett, two of the world's richest men, have publicly stated that they plan to give the bulk of their fortunes to charity. Their children will be comfortably taken care of, no doubt, but neither man believes it is in his family's best interests to inherit billions and billions of dollars. So many billions, in fact, that according to a recent *Money* article, Bill Gates could easily do the following:

- Repair Chicago's public schools for a cost of $3 billion,
- bail out the Russian economy for $12.5 billion,
- fund a manned mission to Mars for $25 billion,
- and *still* have $10.5 billion dollars left over, enough to qualify as the 7th richest person in the United States.

These are mind-boggling sums, sums that can all too easily make your own contributions feel paltry and perhaps unnecessary by comparison. Why do the country's charities need your

$50, $250, or even $500 donation when there are folks like Bill Gates around who could pay for everything?

And it's not just the Gates and the Buffetts who are capable of donating such staggering sums. Joan Kroc of McDonald's recently gave an enormous gift to the Salvation Army—$80 million. Does this mean you don't have to drop money into the red bucket this Christmas?

The nation's charities do need your small donations of money and time. And you need to give your money and time selflessly to them. As women we do seem to have a deep need to take care of others—and what better way than by increasing our net worth, and then being able to take care of even more!

Sadly, even though the past few years of skyrocketing stock market fortunes have created much wealth in the country, fewer households are giving. During this rate of prosperity, the proportion of households that gave charitable contributions dropped to 68.5 percent in 1995 from 71.1 percent in 1987.

As you work your way towards wealth, do not fall into the percentage that does not give of either themselves or their money. Give of yourself to your friends, family, church, and community, and you too will benefit.

We have shared a great deal about the rewards that will come to you once you devote a portion of your time and money to philanthropy. Should you give only because you expect to somehow profit in the end? That sounds so self-centered, it takes away from the spirit of generosity. You must always give without expecting anything in return. We have revealed the theories about tithing and donations only because we want you to understand that this does play a central role in the creation of wealth. But you must give from your heart, not from your calculator.

Don't miss out on your chance to make a difference in the world. Don't miss out on your chance to leave a lasting mark.

EXERCISES

1. Motivational master Mark Victor Hansen shares a great affirmation in his book, *How to Achieve Total Prosperity:* "My prosperity makes everyone better off, and no one worse off." Repeat this affirmation whenever you question whether it is sinful to prosper.

2. Draw up a dream list of charities and the size of the contributions that you would like to give to them. Keep this list with your list of goals and check it occasionally. Send off those checks whenever you can.

3. Draw up a dream list of permanent memorials you'd like to fund—perhaps a scholarship or new building at your alma mater college or high school. Keep this list tucked in with your list of goals as well.

Be Patient in Your Pursuit of Wealth— But Also Be Persistent

Congratulations on reading this book, *The Millionairess Across the Street!* You have shown yourself to be a woman of strength and courage who is passionately devoted to building up her income and net worth, and not willing to sit back and accept second best in life. And with the encouragement and advice of the millionairesses who helped with this book you are well on your way to succeeding. But there is one more trait you must learn—patience.

Yes, patience is important. Your grandmother was right— good things come to those who wait for them (and work like heck to make them happen!). And great success and wealth do not happen overnight. The best type of success, the best type of wealth, is built slowly over the years, one solid step at a time.

What happens when both money and success just fall right into your lap without much effort? Watch out—it will probably not be permanent! There is a peculiar phenomenon that has developed around the country in the wake of legalized lotteries.

All those lucky folks who buck the odds and pick the right numbers and suddenly find themselves with millions of dollars? Well, guess what, most of them lose the money just as quickly. That's right, statistics show that fully three-fifths of lottery winners file for bankruptcy within three years of receiving their windfall! Amazing. Why would this be the case?

Why do most lottery winners blow it all so quickly? Because these are folks who have not been working hard to develop the financial skills it takes to create and manage wealth. These folks have not been patiently working towards goals that they set with a clear understanding of what they wanted to achieve in life. These folks have not laid down the groundwork for long-lasting achievement.

But you will. Through patience and persistence, you will be working to achieve your goals. The goals that you have given great thought to. The goals that fit in with your hopes and dreams. And you know that in order to achieve them, you must be patient.

Remember some of the biographies of famous women that we recommended in Lesson 20? These women did not achieve fame and fortune overnight. Far from it. But yet they persisted, they continued to work patiently towards what they believed in. When asked how she got her start, Madame C.J. Walker, an early cosmetics pioneer replied, "I got a start by giving myself a start." She persisted, and made all of her own opportunities.

The same truth also applies to your career or your business. It takes many years to build lasting skills and the wisdom in your field that will really make you stand out. Overnight career or business success can wreak the same havoc with long-term success that lottery winnings do. If quite suddenly you are a superstar, beneath the gloss and excitement you won't really have the tools to keep building on your success. And you will always feel the nagging doubt that it might all go away just as easily— that you might someday be unmasked as someone who was successful just through a fluke. Be as patient—and persistent—

while building your career success as you must be with your personal wealth.

What if, 12 months after you finish reading this book, your financial picture has not yet improved? Have you failed? Should you just give up and quietly accept what seems to be your lot in life? *No!*

Think of failure as the opportunity to attempt success again, but this time armed with knowledge of what didn't work! And you might as well face the fact now, the more things you attempt in life, the greater the chance that you *will* fail at one or two things. So make failure your friend, and accept that you might be seeing this new friend every few years or so. But don't give up, just keep on trying.

What if, six months from now, you have yet to open an investment account or deposit money into a retirement account? Have you failed there, too? Not yet. You could open the account the very next day. You will begin your journey towards wealth when you are ready to undertake it, not before.

As you develop the patience and persistence to watch your investments build and your career blossom, you will find that slow riches are the most satisfying, and the most long-lived. Over the years you will have learned how long it takes to build up money, and you will develop a newfound respect for money. You also will find yourself less inclined to waste it on frivolous things.

You also must practice patience in your portfolio. Recent studies show that the more frequently an investor makes trades in their portfolio, the lower the return they earn. Better returns are almost always made by the investor who makes solid stock purchases and then leaves them alone to let time and a healthy economy work their magic.

Whenever you feel impatient, return to the list of goals that you have drawn up for yourself. Are you really working the list? Are some of the goals you have chosen things that you can accomplish *without* money? To avoid discouragement, work on a few of those goals for awhile. This will help you keep focused and feel a sense of achievement and momentum.

And when feeling impatient—or worse yet, deflated—close your eyes for a visualization tour into your future, the prosperous future that you are creating. Concentrate on images of success and achievement to get you quickly back on track and feeling upbeat about what the future holds.

Will your friends and family tease you as you plod down the road to future wealth and success? Probably. But do not let it distract you from the goals that you have chosen for yourself. Be sympathetic, as they may well be threatened by the idea that you have set such big goals. Big goals and ideas might scare them personally, and start them wondering if you will leave them behind as you try to achieve your goals.

Julia, a wealthy and successful woman, shared this deeply personal story:

> I'd just read yet another story in the paper about a suddenly successful actor who had dumped his long-time wife for some young thing. As I harrumphed about the indignity of this sort of thing, my husband added his own quiet comment, 'And sometimes successful women leave their husbands behind, too.' His comment really brought me up short. I'd never stopped to think about what kind of an effect my own success would have on him. And in a small way, he was admitting that it was scary.

So while you understand that your family and friends might be threatened, do not allow that to persuade you to abandon the goals you have set.

Once you have achieved both wealth and success, should you quit and just enjoy a life of leisure? You must decide for yourself, but we believe that you should continue to work at the things you enjoy. If your friends and family see you developing into the idle rich, be prepared for real resentment to kick in.

Once someone begins to lead a life that consists only of indulgence, it is all too easy for others to forget just how hard you worked to earn that money.

What do we mean? Just think about Oprah Winfrey, one of the richest women in the country. Do most Americans harbor ill-will towards her for her many millions? Heavens no, they see just how hard she works! How can you resent the good fortunes of someone who not only got their money from working hard, but *continues* to work hard!

We will say it again—*be patient and persistent in your pursuit of wealth*. Do not give up today, do not give up tomorrow. Continue to work towards the dreams that are waiting for you. With patience and persistence, you are cultivating the desire, the talent, the skills, and the knowledge to get exactly what you want.

EXERCISE

Here is a rather zen-like reminder of your goals and the patience you must have while trying to achieve them: Plant a prosperity bush. Choose a fairly young plant from the nursery, one that can represent your goals in their infancy and the great growth that lies ahead.

Plant your new prosperity bush where you can see it several times a day and be reminded of its message.

Care for it as you care for your personal goals, water it and fertilize it to keep it healthy and prospering.

Watch carefully as your new prosperity plant goes through the many cycles of life. Watch it put down new deep roots to support itself as it grows, just as you must.

Watch as it sprouts new growth and reaches for the sun to encourage more activity.

Watch as it sometimes goes through dormant periods, resting during the winter so that it can burst forth again when the sun is warm. You too, will sometimes enter a dormant period on your new path to wealth and success.

And take delight in each new bud, each new flower that sprouts on your prosperity bush, in the same way that each one of your new accomplishments will make you proud and reinvigorate your energy in the long road ahead.

LESSON 23

Enjoy Your Life,
Enjoy Your Money!

The final lesson! After reading 22 different lessons geared towards opening your eyes and changing your thinking about money and success, here you are at last at the end.

But is it really the end? Your journey down the road to building wealth is just beginning, and we would like to share a few final thoughts about the process.

DON'T BECOME CASH-RICH
AND FRIEND-POOR

Every so often you will read in the newspaper about some stingy old person who never spent a dime on themselves, their family, their friends, or their community, and died alone amidst mattresses stuffed with cash. And then there are the stories of friendly folks who used their relatively modest incomes to provide for as many people as they could—starting up programs to help the homeless or buying books for needy children. Sure, the stingy person ended up with more money, but who really had the richer life?

Although we have spent page after page encouraging you to feel confident and unabashed in your pursuit of great wealth, we do not want you to abandon a loving and well-balanced life to do so. Take care to smoothly integrate your financial goals into the rest of your life and not let them push all others to the side. Never put a higher price on the pursuit of money and wealth than on your relationship with your family and friends. Or there you could be, alone in the end, surrounded not by the faces of those who loved you, but by anxious bankers and money-stuffed mattresses.

NEVER FEEL INADEQUATE NEXT TO WEALTHIER FOLKS

Yes, you have decided to build up your net worth and acquire wealth. And in pursuit of that goal we have encouraged you to spend time with all manner of folks who are already more successful financially than you are. Will you feel uncomfortable? We hope not.

You are a valuable and worthy person, regardless of your bank balance. You are a valuable and worthy person, regardless of the car you drive. You are a valuable and worthy person, regardless of the size of your house.

Do not feel that you must fill your life with lots of shiny and expensive objects in order to feel like a part of the crowd. That money is better spent on long-term investments than on a big gold watch or a pair of diamond studs.

Remember to concentrate on discovering *how* these folks became wealthy and successful, not on *how* much money they have now and *how* you can look like you've got it to. Don't overlook the fact that your attempts to look more financially successful than you really are might be easily spotted, and hold you back if your new friends think you are trying to pass yourself off as something that you are not. To present yourself as who you truly are (and where you truly are in life) will get you much farther than a phony attempt to appear as one of the well-heeled.

USE YOUR MONEY FOR LASTING THINGS

And while we are on the topic of avoiding gold watches and diamond earrings, allow us to repeat some of the things we said in Lesson 9 about not squandering your money. We would like to remind you *not to squander your money,* period.

Not only will squandering your money on useless *things* keep you from achieving your financial goals anytime soon, but it also will distract you from what really matters. If you spend your money on things in a mistaken effort to buy love or friendship, or to impress others, you are missing the point of true wealth. Building up wealth can bring you a feeling of security and peace of mind. And of course, it can pay for the occasional fun treat. But too many expensive treats will drain away your resources and leave you back where you began.

Sound too dull for you? Remember, we pulled these strategies together with the idea that they would help you think more powerfully about money. Women can *enjoy* the process of increasing capital and net worth and are *strong enough* to withstand the constant (and we do mean constant) efforts on the parts of others to separate them from their hard-earned money. Women are *confident* enough to take active steps to grow their money. Women *are* millionaires!

500,000 RICH WOMEN—WHO'S NEXT?

There are nearly 500,000 women in the United States who are millionaires. Are *you* next? You can be, if you begin your journey today to *think big now* and *know and believe you deserve to be wealthy!* Don't forget to *take yourself seriously* and *discover your God-given passion.* Get out there and *create your own mastermind group* and work hard to *employ butt-breaking behavior* while you reach for the stars!

Have you started on your *written goals?* They will not only help you define just what you want to accomplish but will remind you to *define yourself by the present and the future, not the past!* And you know how much we want you to *quit squandering your money—keep more to make more.*

Once you have mastered these principles, do everything you can to *get with the wealth boom and join the new economy of ideas*—one that is open to women of all ages, sizes, and economic backgrounds!

Once you *learn all you can about women's wealth and history* and *read and learn all you can about big business,* we hope it will inspire you to get out there and start a business of your own. You will have to *ask, ask, and ask for money again and again* to get your enterprise off the ground, but *don't be shy—build a high profile* to help you get ahead. Just don't *give it away for free!*

And if you don't plan to start your own business, learn to *build wealth without a business* and *don't pay interest—earn it!* Or you can start thinking up ideas that will help you *develop multiple income streams—copyright, patent, and trademark* your way to financial success.

Snuggle up under the covers every night and *read and grow rich—be an information sponge* and learn what you can from the successes (and sometimes failures) of others. But never forget that we are *philanthropists all—be generous with your time and money.*

Most of all, in your pursuit of millionaire status, we remind you to *be patient* in your pursuit of wealth—*but also be persistent.* And *enjoy your life, enjoy your money.*

RESOURCES

ORGANIZATIONS

American Business Women's Association (ABWA)
National Headquarters
9100 Ward Parkway
P.O. Box 8728
Kansas City, MO 64114-0728
816-361-6621
Fax 816-361-4991

This nonprofit organization for working women has 2,100 chapters and 90,000 members. The ABWA offers business education and seminars around the country. Membership includes a subscription to *Women in Business* magazine.

American Women's Economic Development Corporation (AWED)
Headquarters
71 Vanderbilt Avenue, Suite 320
New York, NY 10169
212-692-9100 or 800 222-AWED

West Coast Office
100 West Broadway, Suite 500
Long Beach, CA 90802
310-983-3747
Fax 310-983-3750

Association of Black Women Entrepreneurs
P.O. Box 49368
Los Angeles, CA 90049
213-624-8369

This national organization provides business and educational training, resources, a newsletter, and networking.

Association of Small Business Development Centers
1050 17th Street, NW, Suite 810
Washington, DC 20036
202-887-5599
Fax 202-223-8608

The development centers are located in all states, plus Puerto Rico and the U.S. Virgin Islands. They provide business training and free consulting, as well as programs with an emphasis on international trade.

Business Women's Network (BWN)
1146 19th Street, 3rd Floor
Washington, DC 20036
800-48-WOMEN
Fax 202-833-1808

The BWN offers a directory of women's business organizations in the United States.

Chamber of Commerce

Most cities have a chamber of commerce providing memberships for business networking, training, and education. (Also see National Chamber of Commerce for Women.)

The Committee of 200 (C200)
625 North Michigan Avenue, Suite 500
Chicago, IL 60611
312-751-3477
Fax 312-943-9401

The Committee of 200 is an international organization of leading businesswomen, entrepreneurs, and senior executives of major corporations.

Federation of Organizations for Professional Women (FOWP)
1825 I Street, NW, Suite 400
Washington, DC 20006
202-328-1415

The FOWP offers referral information to entrepreneurs through their bimonthly newsletter and a national directory of women's organizations.

Independent Small Business Employers of America
520 South Pierce Street, Suite 224
Mason City, IA 50401
800-728-3187 or 515-424-3187
Fax 515-424-1673

A membership organization that focuses on helping employers in their role as employers.

International Franchise Association (IFA)
1350 New York Avenue, NW, Suite 900
Washington, DC 20005
202-628-8000
Fax 202-628-0812

A leading source of information about franchising.

Life Plan Center
5 Third Street, Suite 24
San Francisco, CA 94103
415-546-4499
Fax 415-777-1396

Life Plan Center is a nonprofit organization dedicated to men and women over 50 who are in transition in their work and personal lives.

Minority Business Entrepreneur (MBE)
3528 Torrance Boulevard, Suite 101
Torrance, CA 90503-4803
310-540-9398
Fax 310-792-8263
E-mail mbewbe@ix.netcom.com
Web site: www.mbemag.com

National Association of Black Women Entrepreneurs (NABWE)
P.O. Box 1375
Detroit, MI 48231
810-356-3686
Fax 810-354-3793

The NABWE offers meetings and an annual conference.

National Association for Female Executives, Inc. (NAFE)
30 Irving Place
New York, NY 10003
212-477-2200
Fax 212-477-8215

NAFE offers support for female executives and entrepreneurs. Membership includes the magazine *Executive Female,* a venture capital program, loans-by-mail, a career options test, and business publications.

National Association of Women Business Owners (NAWBO)
1100 Wayne Avenue, Suite 830
Silver Springs, MD 20910
301-608-2590
Fax 301-608-2596

NAWBO offers business education through its chapters.

National Chamber of Commerce for Women
10 Waterside Plaza, Suite 6H
New York, NY 10010
212-685-3454

National Education Center for Women in Business (NECWB)
Seton Hill College
Greensburg, PA 15601-1599
412-830-4625 or 800-632-9248
Fax 412-834-7131

National Federation of Black Women Business Owners
1500 Massachusetts Avenue, Suite 34
Washington, DC 20005
202-833-3450
Fax 202-331-7822

National Federation of Business and Professional Women's
  Clubs, Inc., of the United States of America (BPW/USA)
2012 Massachusetts Avenue, NW
Washington, DC 20036
202-293-1100
Fax 202-861-0298

The BPW offers seminars, scholarships for women, and a bimonthly magazine, *National Business Woman*.

National Foundation for Women Business Owners (NFWBO)
1100 Wayne Avenue, Suite 830
Silver Spring, MD 20910
301-495-4975
Fax 301-495-4979
E-mail: nfwbo@worldnet.att.net
Web site: www.nfwbo.org/nfwbo

National Network of Women's Funds
1821 University Avenue, Suite 409N
St. Paul, MN 55104
612-641-0742

National Organization for Women (NOW)
National Headquarters
1000 16th Street, NW, Suite 700
Washington, DC 20036
202-331-0066
Fax 202-785-8576.

U.S. Small Business Administration Office of Women's Business
   Ownership
409 3rd Street, SW
Washington, DC 20416
202-205-6673
E-mail Webmaster www@www.sbaonline.sba.gov
Web site: www.sba.gov/womeninbusiness or www.sba.gov

The programs and resources include training programs, Women's Network for Entrepreneurial Training Mentoring Program, Interagency Committee on Women's Business Enterprise, Women's Prequalification Pilot Loan Program, Federal Procurement Pilot Program for Women-Owned Businesses, and Statistics on Women-Owned Businesses.

U.S. Small Business Administration SBA Answer Desk
800-U-ASK-SBA (800-827-5722)

Call and request The Small Business Directory of publications and videotapes for starting and managing a successful small business.

The White House Office of Women's Initiatives and Outreach
The White House
708 Jackson Place
Washington, DC 20503
202-456-7300
Fax 202-456-7311

This office is a liaison between public and private women's organizations and the administration.

Women in Franchising (WIF)
53 West Jackson Street, Suite 205
Chicago, IL 60604
800-222-4943

An educational, training, and consulting organization that provides information about buying a franchise or starting one from an existing business.

Women Incorporated (WI)
1401 21st Street, Suite 310
Sacramento, CA 95814
800-930-3993 or 916-448-8444
Fax 916-448-8898

WI offers group health insurance, discounts on premier products and services, and access to a loan pool of $150,000,000.

Women's Bureau
U.S. Department of Labor Clearing House on Work and Family
200 Constitution Avenue, NW
Washington, DC 20210
800-827-2700

Women's Business Development Center (WBDC)
8 South Michigan Avenue, Suite 400
Chicago, IL 60603
312-853-3477
Fax 312-853-0145
E-mail wbdccied@aol.com

The WBDC assists women starting or expanding their own business in the greater Chicago area. It also assists other organizations around the country to set up programs.

Women's Work Force Network of Wider Opportunities for Women
    (WOW) and National Commission on Working Women
815 15th Street, NW
Washington, DC 20005
212-638-3143
Fax 202-638-4885

WOW offers business information exchange and leadership development.

Consult your local library for further information about organizations in your area.

BOOKS

Aburdene, Patricia, and John Naisbitt. *Megatrends for Women* (Villard Books, 1992).

Anderson, Nancy. *Work with Passion* (New World Library, 1995).

Arkebauer, James B., with Ron Schultz. *Going Public* (UpStart Publishing, 1994).

Ash, Mary Kay. *Mary Kay—You Can Have It All* (Prima Publishing, 1995).

Basye, Jennifer. *101 Best Extra Income Opportunities for Women* (Prima Publishing, 1997).

Beardstown Ladies' Investment Club. *Beardstown Ladies' Common-Sense Investment Guide* (Hyperion, 1994).

———. *Beardstown Ladies' Guide to Smart Spending for Big Savings* (Hyperion, 1997).

Beauchamp, Cari. *Without Lying Down: Frances Marion and the Powerful Women of Early Hollywood* (Scribner, 1997).

Bollier, David. *Aiming Higher* (AMACOM, 1996).

Briles, Judith, PhD, Edwin C. Schilling III, DD, CFP, and Carol Ann Wilson, CFP, CDP. *The Dollars and Sense of Divorce* (Dearborn Financial Publishing, 1998).

Bykofsky, Sheree, and Jennifer Basye Sander. *The Complete Idiot's Guide to Getting Published* (Alpha Books, 1998).

Case, Samuel. *The First Book of Investing* (Prima Publishing, 1994).

Clason, George S. *Richest Man in Babylon* (New American Library, 1997).

Collins-Felton, Victoria, PhD, CFP. *Couples and Money* (Bantam, 1990, 1992; Nolo, 1998).

Costello, Cynthia, and Barbara Kivimae Krimgold, eds. *American Woman 1996–97* (W.W. Norton, 1996).

Cuthbertson, Ken. *Nobody Said Not to Go: The Life, Loves, and Adventures of Emily Hahn* (Faber & Faber, 1998).

Debelak, Don. *Entrepreneur Magazine: Bringing Your Product to Market* (John Wiley & Sons, 1997).

Deep, Samuel D., and Lyle Sussman. *Smart Moves for People in Charge* (Addison-Wesley, 1995).

Degeorge, Gail. *The Making of a Blockbuster* (John Wiley & Sons, 1995).

Devine, William Francis. *Women, Men & Money* (Harmony Books, 1998).

Dreizler, Bob. *Tending Your Money Garden* (Rossonya Books, 1998).

Edelman, Ric. *The Truth about Money* (Georgetown University Press, 1996).

Englander, Debra Wishik. *How to Be Your Own Financial Planner* (Prima Publishing, 1996).

Fitzgerald, Judith. *Building a Mystery: The Story of Sarah McLachlan & Lilith Fair* (Quarry, 1998).

Flores, Bettina R. *Chiquita's Cocoon* (Villard Books, 1994; Pepper Vine Press, 1997).

Gilberd, Pamela Boucher. *Eleven Commandments of Wildly Successful Women* (Macmillan Spectrum, 1996).

Graham, Katharine. *Personal History* (Knopf, 1997).

Hall, Stephen F., *From Kitchen to Market* (Upstart Publishing, 1996).

Herera, Sue. *Women of the Street: Making It on Wall Street* (John Wiley & Sons, 1997).

Hill, Napolean. *Think and Grow Rich* (Fawcett, 1990).

Husch, Tony, and Linda Foust. *That's a Great Idea* (Ten Speed Press, 1987).

Jaffe, Azriela. *Honey, I Want to Start My Own Business* (HarperBusiness, 1996).

Jones, Star. *You Have to Stand for Something or You'll Fall for Anything* (Bantam, 1998).

Karasik, Paul. *How to Make It Big in the Seminar Business* (McGraw Hill, 1992).

Kaye, Evelyn. *Amazing Traveler: Isabella Bird* (Blue Panda, 1994).

Klepper, Michael, and Robert Gunther. *The Wealthy 100* (Citadel Press Book, 1996).

Macdonald, Anne L., *Feminine Ingenuity* (Ballantine Books, 1992).

Markham. Beryl. *West with the Night* (North Point Press, 1985).

Mellan, Olivia. *Overcoming Overspending* (Walker & Co., 1995).

Mitchell, Margaret. *Gone with the Wind* (Macmillan, 1996).

Nemeth, Maria, PhD. *You and Money* (Vildehiya Publications, 1997).

Norman, Jan. *What No One Ever Tells You about Starting Your Own Business* (Dearborn Financial Publishing, 1998).

O'Hara, Thomas E., and Kenneth S. Janke, Sr. *Starting and Running a Profitable Investment Club* (Times Books, 1998).

O'Neill, Barbara. *Saving on a Shoestring* (Dearborn Financial Publishing, 1995).

Pinson, Linda, and Jerry Jinnett. *Anatomy of a Business Plan* (Upstart Publishing, 1996).

Ponder, Catherine. *The Dynamic Laws of Prosperity* (Prentis Hall, 1962).

Randall, Margaret. *The Price You Pay* (Routledge, 1996).

Read, Phyllis J., and Bernard L. Witlieb. *The Book of Women's Firsts* (Random House, 1992).

Rubin, Harriet. *The Princessa* (Dell Publishing, 1997).

Schor, Juliet. *The Overspent American* (Basic Books, 1998).

Schulz, Howard, and Dori Jones Yanq. *Pour Your Heart into It* (Hyperion, 1997).

Schwartz, David J., PhD, *The Magic of Thinking Big* (Fireside, 1959).

Sexton, Donald L., and Raymond W. Smilor, eds. *Entrepreneurship 2000* (Upstart Publishing, 1997).

Shirley, Kay R., PhD, CFP, *Live Long and Profit* (Dearborn Financial Publishing, 1997).

Stanley, Thomas J., PhD, and William D. Danko, PhD. *The Millionaire Next Door* (Longstreet Press, 1996).

Steel, Dawn. *They Can Kill You, but They Can't Eat You* (Pocket Books, 1993).

Trager, James. *The Women's Chronology* (Henry Holt and Company, 1994).

Wallach, Janet. *Desert Queen* (Doubleday, 1996).

Walters, Dottie, and Lilly Walters. *Speak and Grow Rich* (Prentice Hall, 1989).

Walton, Sam. *Sam Walton: Made in America* (Bantam, 1993).

Yudkin, Marcia. *Six Steps to Free Publicity* (Plume, 1994).

MAGAZINES

Most of these magazines and others can be found in your local bookstore as well as online.

Barron's
Bloomberg
Business Start-Ups
Business 2.0
Business Week
Entrepreneur
Essence
Fast Company
Forbes
Fortune
Hispanic Inc.: The Magazine for Growing Companies.

Income Opportunities
Nation's Business: The Small Business Advisor
Success: The Magazaine for Today's Entrepreneurial Mind
Variety
Working Mother
Working Woman

MISCELLANEOUS RESOURCES

Patent and Trademark Office
Commissioner of Patents and
   Trademarks
Washington, DC 20231

Patent and Trademark Office
The Scientific and Technical
   Information Center
2021 Jefferson Davis Highway
Arlington, VA 22202
703-557-2957

Patent Information
   Clearinghouse
Sunnyvale Public Library
665 West Olive Avenue
Sunnyvale, CA 94088-3714
408-730-7290

Patent Depository
Los Angeles Public Library
630 West Fifth Street
Los Angeles, CA 90071-2097
213-612-3273

Complete patent depository.

Patent Depository
San Diego Public Library
820 E Street
San Diego, CA 92101-6478
619-236-5813

Patents since 1951.

Patent Depository
California State Library
914 Capital Mall
Sacramento, CA 95814
916-654-0069

Patents since 1960.

U.S. Department of Commerce
Trade Information Center
800-USA-TRADE

Can fax you information on ex-
porting to various countries.

Consumer Information
   Catalogue
Pueblo, CO 81009
888-8-PUEBLO (888-878-3256)
Fax: 719-948-9724
Web site: www.pueblo.gsa.gov

Free catalogs on almost any
subject.

INDEX